I Was Lost
But Now I'm
Found

I Was Lost But Now I'm Found

JAMILA DOXY - JOHNSON

I Was Lost But Now I'm Found

Copyright © 2024 by Jamila Doxy - Johnson. All rights reserved.

No part of this publication may be reproduced, stored in a retrieval system or transmitted in any way by any means, electronic, mechanical, photocopy, recording or otherwise without the prior permission of the author except as provided by USA copyright law.

The opinions expressed by the author are not necessarily those of URLink Print and Media.

1603 Capitol Ave., Suite 310 Cheyenne, Wyoming USA 82001
1-888-980-6523 | admin@urlinkpublishing.com

URLink Print and Media is committed to excellence in the publishing industry.

Book design copyright © 2024 by URLink Print and Media. All rights reserved.

Published in the United States of America

Library of Congress Control Number: 2024923446
ISBN 978-1-68486-975-6 (Paperback)
ISBN 978-1-68486-979-4 (Digital)

25.10.24

CONTENTS

Acknowledgements 7
Introduction 9
Why Me, Lord? 11
The Messenger 17
The First Date 24
The Dream of a Savior 29
He Loves Me, He Loves Me Not 31
Our Lunch Date 37
Broken-Hearted 42
The Secret's Out 45
The Meeting 51
Love at First Sight 54
Halloween Bash 58
The Parent's Introduction 62
Will and Jada Smith Wannabes 68
Psychic Talk 72
The Big Day 77
The Holidays 80
Two of a Kind 82
The Exorcism 86
Stirring Up the Gift 95
The Time Has Come 98
A New Beginning 108
Mr. Khalil's Arrival 113
Calling 117
The Breakup 122

ACKNOWLEDGEMENTS

To my Lord Jesus Christ, my Savior:
I thank you for opening up my heart to the TRUTH! You have brought me out of darkness to a life full of light.

Your light shines on me every morning, even on the rough days.

My faith in you has brought me closer to you Lord, and I am forever thankful to have in my possession a growing and intimate relationship with you.

I praise you for redirecting me back on life's path of righteousness.

Thank you for this new life.

Love always.

My heart goes out to those who struggle with mental illness. You are not alone on this journey. I can relate. Sometimes the walk is a challenge; however, I want you to know God loves you, and He sees your struggle. Open your heart and let Jesus in to Heal you.

"Our deepest fear is not that we are inadequate.

Our deepest fear is that we are powerful beyond measure. It is our light, not our darkness that most frightens us. We ask ourselves, Who am I to be brilliant, gorgeous, talented, fabulous?

Actually, who are you not to be? You are a child of God. Your playing small does not serve the world. There is nothing enlightened about shrinking so that other people won't feel insecure around you. We are all meant to shine, as children do. We were born to make manifest the glory of God that is within us. It's not just in some of us; it's in everyone. And as we let our own light shine, we unconsciously give other people permission to do the same. As we are liberated from our own fear, our presence automatically liberates others."

—Marianne Williamson

INTRODUCTION

I know you are thinking to yourself oh boy, here is another author telling me what to do. To be honest, that's not the purpose of this book. My purpose of this book is to reveal the TRUTH.

Have you ever felt like something was stopping you from succeeding in life? Every time you get on track, something derails you off your path to success. When you get the motivation to accomplish your goals, you begin to discover the power within. You feel powerful enough to conquer the world, but something distracts you. You get discouraged, and you quit. I once felt the same way until I realized that I had to pay less attention to the physical and more attention to the spiritual world around me.

What I'm about to reveal to you is something you should take seriously. It can help you think beyond the current obstacles in your life for good.

PLEASE PAY ATTENTION.

WHY ME, LORD?

My heart is pounding, and my palms are sweating. What is going on? My mind is racing. I cannot control it; I cannot control these thoughts. Is this a dream?

It seems so real.

Stop!

Please stop!

Oh no!

I can see now. He is living another life. He is living a life of lies and deception.

Wait!

What is this strange eerie feeling in my chest? It is getting stronger and stronger.

Why won't this stop?

Where is this going?

I can see what he has done. It is another woman that I see. She lives upstairs in the attic. The woman at the job. The woman at the store. Who are all these women?

"He is going to leave with her. The voice said. He is a liar. Kick him out now."

Sarah said this would happen. Why didn't I believe her?

Who is Sarah?

Sarah is a woman who help saved my life. She is a messenger from God who led me out of bondage. As I look back on that night, a night of terror, I did not know that night was the beginning of a beautiful transformation, a transformation that had taken me from a life of darkness to a life full of light. That was the first time I realized there was much more to life than what I was seeing with my human eyes. That was also the first time I ever heard the voice of Satan.

It all began about three years ago, in the fall of 2009 when I was sitting on the edge of my bed crying hysterically, wondering why my life had turned out so badly. I hated everything about myself. My self-esteem was so low that I didn't want to exist anymore. I didn't want to face the hardships of life. My perspective on life was completely negative. Negativity surrounded me. I had begun to think that this was all there was to life, always struggling to overcome negative obstacles. I thought, "Who wants to be happy all the damn time!"

My attitude was so negative and I hated those who brought any positive energy into my negative circle. My life consisted of drama, but even though my life was so negative, it was still exciting! It was not boring like those religious people's lives. Those Christians were too holy for me! Those Muslims were too strict for me!

I was raised in the church as a Christian since I was born. However, when I was thirteen, my brother introduced me to Islam. God had allowed me to have a change of heart towards my belief. I was so intrigued by the power and organization that I wanted to join the Nation of Islam. All I wanted to be more than anything in the world was to be a Muslim, but my mother would not hear of it. The rule was as long as I stayed under her roof, I WAS A CHRISTIAN. I had fallen in love with the discipline and organization of Islam, but not

God. My mom, brother, and I lived on the south side of Chicago for the first fifteen years of my life. After my parents divorced, my mother remarried, and in 1997, we moved to the south suburbs of Illinois in a little town called Country Club Hills.

Growing up as a kid on the South Side of Chicago was a challenge but my mom and dad made sure my brother and I were safe and well taken care of. They called the neighborhood which I lived in the 'wild wild hundreds. The wild wild hundreds were at the time a violent neighborhood. There was always a war between the street gangs in my neighborhood. I remember seeing gang members with coats on in the summertime. I know you are saying to yourself WHY? Well if a gang was about to retaliate against a rival gang then the gang members would wear coats to hide the guns. Just know you did not want to be outside when you saw them running down the streets with coats on.

As a kid I was very observant but loved to play outside. Playing outside was one of my passions. Sometimes I use to eat my dinner outside on the front porch. My friends and I played many games. We played house, school Mr. freeze, baseball, and kick ball. We used to have so much fun playing with one another. On the other hand, we experienced some hard ache and pain. One of my childhood best friends was shot. Anthony Currie is his name. We were two peas in a pod. We talked about everything. As I look back, he truly was my first male best friend. The day I was told he got shot, I could actually feel my stomach drop. My eyes watered and tears came down my face. I was at least 10 or 11 years old when this happened. That was the day I realized what type of neighborhood I was living in. I was tired of the violence. I was tired of the gangs retaliating against each other. Our block was one of the war zones for the gangs. When the gangs retaliated against each other, it seemed like they never could shoot the right target. There were too many stand byers getting killed. Most of the stand byers were children.

Although we lived in a violent neighborhood, everyone on the block always looked forward to the block club party each summer. My mother was the captain of the block club party. I used to wake up early anticipating the time to arrive for me, my bother Eugene, my niece Krystle, my nephew Rasheed and my sister Kim to go outside for the block club party. My mother would order a huge bounce house. Different neighbors on the block would volunteer to cook. This particular year my mom was letting me perform a song. The song was Tomorrow by Tevin Campbell. I was so nervous that day, but I sung that song with all of my little heart. Everyone on the block cheered me on and congratulated me for being so brave to get up there to sing. I felt so courageous. After the entertainment was the games, oh boy we had a ball. There was one particular game I enjoyed seeing the older kids play. It was called the dress race game. There were two teams and each person on the team had to put on a set of clothes, a pair of shoes, hat, and a wig. They had to run to the destination and run back where they began. Then they had to undress and give everything to the next person in line. That was my favorite game. It was so funny to see everybody come together and have a good time. Our block parties were so fun even the gang members on the block had to participate.

I also remember the year when me and my friends performed a dance to the song by Luke Doo Doo brown. Oh boy we were too hot, but someone special noticed our behavior. We were always dancing in a provocative way. We learned to dance by watching provocative videos. Like I said someone special was watching us. Her name was Amelia. She lived across the street from my family and me. One day while we were dancing on my front porch, Ms. Amelia had begun to walk towards us. I noticed her and turned off the music. She began to tell us how young ladies should behave and dress. She went on to ask us if we wanted to meet and go out sometimes. We were so excited, and we all said yes. We met every week. Sometimes on the weekend we went to out to eat. Our group was named S.U.G.A.R. (Sisters Under God's Authority and Rules). Amelia had dropped a powerful seed in my soul. Amelia got married and moved away. Unfortunately, S.U.G.A.R ended.

As I grew older, my parents divorced. I guess my mother had gotten tired of the arguments and fights. My father was diagnosed with schizophrenia. Sometimes he wouldn't take his medicine and that's when the paranoia kicked in. After my father moved out, I was very sad. Our home wasn't the same when my father moved out. I missed his laughter and smile. Most importantly, I missed the family traditions. One of my favorite traditions was family pizza night. Every Friday My dad and I would go to the neighborhood store to buy pizza set ups. The pizza package came with the crust, sauce, cheese, and sausage. The time I spent with my dad was priceless.

Although my dad struggled with mental Illness, he has a heart of gold. In my eyes my dad did no wrong. He was my protector. Our relationship changed tremendously when my dad got remarried. As a teenager I wanted my dad to myself. I didn't want to share my dad's time. As time went on, I began to look for attention from guys

I thank God for my mother for providing me with a strong foundation in Christianity and for being stern with me. If I would have known then what I know now, I would have recognized a lie when it was presented to me, but like I said, God had granted me to have a change of heart toward Christianity. I was on this assignment for fourteen years. Unfortunately, I had to spend most of my teenage through adult years wrestling with the confusion of where the truth was. Who holds the ultimate truth, the Muslims or the Christians? During this search for the truth, I had lost myself and most of my life experiences were hurtful, which slowly but surely pushed me away from God. My mind was full of lies and I became rebellious. I felt God owed me since I had experienced so much hurt.

This state of mind I was in was destroying my life. Within the last three years, my life had changed drastically. I was so angry with God. How could God let these terrible things happen to me? I wanted to know where this mysterious God was when I was molested as a little girl. Where was God when my father rejected me? Where was God when I endured verbal and physical abuse from men in past relationships, and where was he when my marriage fell? Every time a question crossed my mind, the more furious I became with God. I felt used and abused, and I wanted to give up on life.

My life continued heading in the wrong direction. I knew something was wrong. I used to hear the voice of the Lord when I was a child. *Why couldn't I hear God's voice any longer?* I questioned myself. The hurt from the past was tormenting me. I thought God had turned his back on me. I wanted all the pain in the past to stop. There were nights that I prayed, "Lord, make it stop; the pain is too strong. Lord, please take away the pain." Continuing to cry, I would get on my knees and ask God to send me help. I knew something was wrong, but I couldn't put my finger on it. The world didn't seem real. I felt I belonged somewhere else. After I cried out for help, I cried myself to sleep.

THE MESSENGER

October 17, 2008, was the day my life began to change. That morning I woke up with a different attitude. I was happy. I told my six-year-old son that we were going out to eat. I was separated from my husband, and the other guy I was dating was a manipulator he basically ended our little fling and tossed me to the side. As I was getting ready for the exciting outing, I could feel those thoughts of sadness. It was a void, an emptiness that I have been carrying for years. I tried to fill that void with men, but the men I chose were selfish and abusive. Having to come back to live with my mom was also depressing. I was on my own with my fiancée at the time, but differences had broken up our union.

During that time, if I could rate my self-esteem from one to ten, I would rate myself at a zero. I didn't think I deserved a good man. There were so many things going wrong in my life, and my friend's life wasn't any better. My surroundings were negative; plus, I was dealing with this eerie feeling of being different. Don't get me wrong—I love my family dearly, but every time I was around them, I felt like the outcast. I felt like I didn't belong.

"Mom, is you ready?" my son Jalon shouted as he knocked on the bathroom door, interrupting my thoughts of sadness.

"Just about, honey. Go have a seat in the living room while I get ready."

"Okay," he responded.

As we drove to Applebee's, which is Jalon's favorite restaurant, those depressing thoughts arrived again. *You messed up your marriage. Another failed relationship. Don't anybody want you now.* Day by day, the guilt was stripping my self-esteem.

HONK, HONK! Suddenly I grabbed the steering wheel and turned left trying to refrain from hitting the car in my right lane. My heart jumped. "Pay attention, Jamila!" I shouted. I looked in the rearview mirror to make sure Jalon was okay. Luckily, he was asleep. I was relieved. *Thank God he didn't witness his mother being an irresponsible wreck*, I thought.

Finally we arrived to Applebee's. As soon as the car stopped, Jalon woke up I guess the aroma of the food had awakened him. One of Jalon's favorite things to do is EAT! He was so delighted to finally be at the restaurant. Although I was dressed to impress and I had a smile on my face, on the inside I was hurting, hurting bad. This continuous emotional and dreadful hurt was getting to be unbearable. I had eaten so much food thinking the fullness of my stomach would suppress some of the emotional turmoil I was experiencing.

RING, RING! I reached into my purse to find my phone, but no luck. "Mom it's in your pocket," Jalon said.

"Hello," I said in a mysterious voice, trying to recognize this man's voice.

"Hi, so are we still on for tonight?" "Oh, hi, how are you doing?"

"I'm good."

"Oh, the movies, right?"

"Uh, yeah."

By his response, it sounded like he was a little irritated because he had figured out that I had forgotten about our date.

"You know what? I have many things I need to do, so I don't know about the movies. I will have to call you back in about twenty minutes. I have to confirm with my babysitter."

"Oh, okay. Well, let me know what you are going to do."

"Okay, I will definitely let you know. Bye."

"Bye."

"Mom, who was that?" Jalon asked as soon as I got off the phone. He was smiling with ketchup all over his mouth. Little boys can be so protective of their moms.

"Oh, just a friend. Now, you finish eating your food and take your time eating. Quick stuffing your mouth." Changing the subject and redirecting his focus off of the person who was on the phone was my intentions. I didn't want to talk about or introduce my son to any other men. He had been through enough with the men I had been dating. Plus, the fact I was going through a divorce didn't make it any better.

After our stomachs were full and satisfied, I paid the bill and we slowly walked to the car looking like some stuffed pigs. As I drove home, those depressing thoughts crept back in my mind. All I could concentrate on was my failures. Of course I had some positive accomplishments, but my mind wanted to focus on the negatives.

Within two blocks of our home, tears began to run down my face. Immediately I looked in the rearview mirror to see if Jalon was paying attention to me. Again and thankfully, he was fast asleep. Sitting at the red traffic light, I had a weird moment, but this weird moment wasn't foreign to me. It had happened to me numerous times. It was like my mind had gone into a trance. For about ten seconds my mind had gone somewhere else. To a place of peace.

HONK, HONK! The sound of the horn from the car behind me snapped me out of it. As I proceeded to make my left turn, I saw a sign on my left that read "Psychic Readings." I pulled over and dialed the number.

"Hello, hi, I was just driving and I saw your sign. Can I come in to get a reading?"

"Oh, of course, sweetie. Please come in," the woman. responded.

"Okay, bye."

"Jalon, wake up, baby. Come on. We're making a quick stop." Excited and afraid at the same time, I led us up to the door of a small house. Before I could knock on the door, a short full-figured Hispanic woman walked to the door.

"Please come in," she said. As we walked in, I saw three children in the living room watching television. Interrupting my observation of my surroundings, she greeted Jalon and me.

"Hi. My name is Sarah and these are my children." I don't recall their names, but they were small children between three and six years old.

"My name is Jamila, and this is my son Jalon."

Turning to Jalon, I said, "Jalon, say 'hi."

In a quiet shy voice he responded, "Hi." Quickly, he redirected his focus to the kids giving me the innocent puppy eyes, waiting for my permission so he could join the kids.

Sarah directed me to the kitchen. "Have a seat. I'll be with be you in a few."

I was so nervous. I had heard about these psychics on television, but I never met this type of person in real life. *I wonder what they see. How does this psychic thing work? Where does this magical power come from?* I thought to myself as I waited patiently for her to reenter the kitchen. I wanted to ask her so many questions, but fear invaded my mind and killed the thoughts.

"Sorry for the wait," she said as she entered the kitchen. "So, what brings you in today?"

"I want a reading."

"Well, do you want a full-reading or a half-reading? It's twenty dollars for a half-reading and thirty-five for a full-reading."

"I'll go with the half-reading." As she placed the deck of cards on the table, the thoughts of curiosity crossed my mind. *I wonder if she really is a psychic or is she going to read off of my questions.*

"First of all, I want to explain to you that my gift is a gift from God. This gift is real, and I use this gift to help others who cross my path. I want you to relax. You have nothing to fear. What I want you to do is pick a card from the deck."

As I reached for the card, I felt an uncomfortable feeling in my chest. "Are you ready?" she asked.

"Yes," I said in a hesitant tone.

The card I picked had a person on it dressed in clothing.

"This is a high card. It's a holy card. You have a promising future. A future of wealth and fame awaits you, but you are being blocked."

"Being blocked by what?" I asked in a soft but irritated tone.

"You are being blocked by a guy that you can't stop thinking about. This man is not from God and he doesn't respect you. He thinks you are weak and loves to control you. You are also being blocked by fear. You are so fearful of this man. This man is not from God and you need to remove him from your life completely."

"I'm not with him anymore."

"You may not be with him, but you have to get rid of everything in your house that reminds you of him. Get rid of everything fast! Not only is this man blocking you from your success, but he is also blocking you from meeting your soul mate."

My eyes grew big. "So, there really is a such thing as a soul mate?"

"Yes," she said. "We all have one, and most of us spend a lifetime searching for our soul mate, but you have been blessed with yours."

"Well, where is he?" I asked, smiling and looking at her with enthusiasm.

"He has been around you a couple of times. He's at your job. He's tall and he has a brown complexion."

Immediately, his face popped into my mind. Is it him, the one I've been dreaming about? The one I've been praying and writing about since I was eleven years old. All these thoughts were playing in my mind as I continued to visualize his face.

"I have a date with him tonight." I was getting so excited. "To be honest, I don't want to deal with another man in my life. I have had it with men. I thought about canceling the date. I really don't want to be bothered."

"No, don't do that. Remember, this is your soul mate. Get excited, girl. Get rid of that other man completely from your mind and get dressed up and go on this date. This will be the start of a new beginning for you and him.

Go out and enjoy yourself. Also, I want you to come back next week. What day is good for you?"

"Any day is good for me next week as long as the time is after 2:30 p.m."

"Great! Let's schedule our next meeting on Tuesday at 3:00 p.m. of this coming week."

"That works for me!" I said in excitement. "It was so nice to meet you."

As I gave her a quick handshake, she looked at me as if she were holding more information from me. I wanted to ask her if there was something else she needed to tell me, but I was eager to get home and relax.

"All right, Jalon, it's time to go."

"Aww, Mom, but I watching TV," he said in a whining tone.

"Jalon, come on. We have to go." He grabbed his hat and slowly walked to the front door. I turned around to face Sarah.

"Well, I'll see you next week on Tuesday at 3 p.m.," I said while waiting for confirmation. By the way she was looking at me; I could tell she was still reading me. She was keeping something from me.

"You got it. Next Tuesday at 3 p.m.," she responded, confirming my look.

THE FIRST DATE

As Jalon and I pulled out of the driveway, I was so excited and curious to hear what Sarah was going to say next week. *What is she keeping from me?* I thought to myself. *Is it something bad or good?* At that moment it felt good to be part of something I could relate to. Sarah and I had something in common. She was different from the norm and so was I. I hadn't identified my uniqueness yet. To be honest, I was afraid to find out my own unique quality. I knew I was on to something by going to see this psychic, but she wasn't what I had expected. I expected her to be this 'mysterious and magical being'; instead, she seemed to be a normal human being except, of course, for this unique gift of knowledge.

Jalon and I finally made it home, and I was ready to relax. While giving Jalon his bath, all I could think about was the conversation about my future, and my soul mate.

RING, RING! My cell phone interrupted my thoughts. I ran out of the bathroom and I nearly hurt myself tripping over one of Jalon's shoes. I searched for the phone and hoped that it was him, my soul mate *oh, my goodness, could this be true? Have I finally found my true love that I've been searching for since the age eleven?*

Finally I discovered my phone in my purse buried under layers of unimportant papers.

"Oh, my goodness, it's him!" I said in excitement, trying to keep my composure so I could finally answer the phone.

"Hello?"

"Hi."

"Hi, what's going on?"

"Are we still on for tonight?"

"Of course," I said. "What movie theater are we meeting at?"

"Oh, we can meet at the Country Club Hills Lowes Theater around your house. Is that okay?"

"That's perfect! Call me when you get on the expressway."

"All right, bye!

"Bye." I hurried and hung up the phone and began dancing in the mirror singing "I have a date.' I couldn't stop dancing in the mirror. Suddenly, the fear began to overwhelm my mind. *What if he turns out to be like those other men who have abused me in the past?* I thought to myself. *I can't take any more disappointments. He seems to be a nice guy, but looks can be deceiving.* I became nervous and sadden. Being hurt again by another man was all I needed to push me over the edge.

"He's your soul mate." The voice of Sarah interrupted those negative thoughts and a smiled crossed my face.

"Wow, what if he truly is my soul mate? The one I dreamed about six months ago. The one I've been waiting for. The one God made and set aside just for me. What a beautiful thing for a person to experience. There are so many people out there that don't get the chance to be with their soul mate; instead they get impatient and settle for whatever feels right at the time."

"Jamila, who are you talking to?" The voice of my mom interrupted my intimate conversation with myself as she entered my room.

"Oh, I was talking to myself." She had a strange look on her face.

"Well, honey, have a nice time, and you look beautiful. You've been through so much in the last couple of years. I just want you to be happy."

My mother has always been supportive of me. She is loving and encouraging. How I love her dearly and how blessed I am to have her as my mother.

"Are you going to church tomorrow?" she asked.

"Uh, no!"

"Why not?"

"I'll go when it's time for me to go." With the look of disappointment upon her face, she kissed me on the cheek.

"MOM, MOM, I'M READY! Jalon yelled from the bathroom. I had almost forgotten the boy was still in the tub.

"I'll go get him," my mom said.

"Mom, you're the best." I kissed her in return and finished getting ready.

RING, RING! "Where is this stupid phone? Why can't I ever find this damn phone when I need it?" It was in my coat pocket.

Oh, wow, it's him; here goes nothing.

"Hello. Jamila?"

"Yes, this is me."

"Hi. I'm exiting 167th just as we speak."

"Okay, I'll be leaving in two minutes. I'll be there around 8:30 p.m."

"What time does the movie start again?"

"It starts at 9:00 p.m.," I told him. The plan was for us to meet at least thirty minutes earlier, so we could engage in conversation. "I'll be leaving now."

Although I wasn't completely ready, he didn't need to know that. I only had to curl one more strand of hair, put on my earrings, and then I would be ready. As I sprayed on my favorite mist by Victoria's Secret, I visualized us having a happy future together.

Okay, Jamila, you are going too fast. Calm down. This is you guys' first date. Wow, my soul mate. Okay, snap out of it, Jamila. I grabbed my coat and headed out.

"Come here, honey, and give me a kiss," I said to Jalon. "Be good with Grandma, okay?"

He kissed me on the check and said, "Have a good time, Mom." Those words touched my heart coming from my six-year-old son, whose voice calms me and brings me serenity. For a second, the thought of staying at home with him surfaced my mind, but a date with my soul mate was also appealing to me, so out the door I went.

When I pulled up to the movie theater, the feelings of nervousness kicked in. My heart began to race and my palms began to sweat. I felt like a nervous high school teenager going on her first date. I took a couple of deep breaths.

Here goes nothing. I got out of the car and began walking to the theater. *I wonder if he is in his car watching me walk into the theater. Jamila, clam down. You are going to scare the poor man off.* Talking to myself was a technique I used whenever I was nervous. My mouth was parched. I entered the doors to the theater.

RING, RING!

"Hello, Jamila, did you make here yet?"

"Yes, I just walked in."

"Where are you?" he asked. As I looked over, I saw him looking and finally his eyes met my eyes. I walked over to him in line.

"Hi."

"What's up! You look nice."

"And so do you." I looked him up and down. Wow, be is tall and fine I can work with this, I thought to myself. He brought our tickets and we headed to the theater.

"Thanks," he said.

I really don't care for scary movies, but we watched *The Edge of Darkness*. He made comments about the movie, but I was thinking about the "soul mate" thing, so I didn't laugh at his jokes. I wasn't being rude, but I couldn't grasp the idea that I was sitting next to my soul mate. *Wow*, I thought to myself.

I couldn't wait to meet with Sarah again and tell her about our first date. I was so busy focusing on the fact of him being my soul mate that I didn't get a chance to enjoy the moment. After the movie, we went into the lobby. We sat there talking. Well, he did all the talking; I just listened. I was so sleepy that I had begun to yawn frequently.

I wonder what he is thinking right now. I hope he doesn't think I'm not interested because I'm yawning, I thought to myself. I was so nervous that night that I couldn't enjoy the moment. We said our good-byes and departed. As I was driving home, his face popped into my mind. I couldn't get this man off my mind, yet at the same time I wanted to tell him that I wasn't ready for anything serious. I didn't want to be bothered with any man. I just wanted to have fun with him while it lasted. All those exciting thoughts of him being my soul mate were replaced with fear. Getting home to Jalon became my main concern.

I was so sleepy walking in the house and I rushed into the bed. As I drifted off to sleep, thoughts of him crossed my mind again and I smiled. Falling asleep with a smile is a great way to end the night.

THE DREAM OF A SAVIOR

It is pitch dark and I try to open my eyes, but something is forcing them shut. I try to move, but I can't move a muscle. I am being controlled. I can hear and feel something moving around me. Finally, I force my eyes open. As I look around, I see these demonic beings walking around checking on the robots. Inside of the robots are people. As I look down at my hands, I realize that I am one of them, a robot being controlled. Again, I glance around me and everybody seems to be in a deep sleep. I am the only one who is awake. All of the sudden, one of the demonic beings heads my way. I hurry and close my eyes, wishing that my curiosity didn't open them. I can feel its breath on my face. Finally, I don't feel its presence anymore and I open my eyes. As I open my eyes, the demonic being turns around and we make eye contact. I try to run, but I can't move. It's coming at me at full force.

It's going to kill me.

◆

I woke up screaming, and I was drenched in sweat. I had to catch my breath. That dream made me feel uneasy. If I wasn't mistaken, I have had this dream before. I wonder what it means. I wonder what he is doing, I thought to myself as I changed my clothes. It was very hard for me to go back to sleep.

HE LOVES ME, HE LOVES ME NOT

The next morning, I was tired as hell. It was difficult for me to let the bed go on this Monday morning. Realizing I only had gotten about four hours of sleep, I was eager to call off from work. I began to think of reasons to get out of bed and go to work. *Maybe he will be a substitute teacher at our school today or maybe he will be assigned to the classroom I am working in.* The thought of him pushed me out of bed, and I walked in Jalon's room.

Smiling and looking at my son sleeping peacefully with his thumb in his mouth, I had begun to reminisce and visualize when he was a baby. He was so fat and beautiful. Pushing out an eight pounds, six ounces baby was all worth it. He is such a wonderful kid, and I love him dearly. Jalon and I have been through some rough times, but he still remains so peaceful and loving. I glanced at my watch and realized time was ticking.

"Jalon, sweetheart, it's time for you to get up. Come on, honey. Get up."

"Aw, Mom, I don't want to get up." Of course he takes after his mom, and we're not morning people at all. "I know, honey; your bed is comfortable, isn't it?" He nodded.

"Well, Jalon," I said, "before you know it, it will be Friday again, so let's get up and get the day started." He eventually got up and I made us breakfast. Together we sat at the table and ate our breakfast. Jalon loves to eat and he slowly began to come out of his little mood swing.

"Mom, can I have some more oatmeal?"

"No, honey, we are running out of time. I need you to go brush your teeth and get dressed so we can get out of here on time. "This job wasn't the best paying job, but it was right down the street from my house, plus Jalon went to school in the district where I worked as a classroom aide for special education students. Even though we were at different schools, knowing that we were only two blocks away from each other gave me a sense of comfort as an attached mother.

Finally, we headed out the door and began our day. As I pulled up to the school, I glanced over and parked next to me was my soul mate's truck. Instantly, a smile appeared on my face. *Oh, my goodness, he's here.* Butterflies filled the pit of my stomach. I pulled out my lip gloss and comb to add the finishing touches of my beauty. I was nervous, but excited at the same time. I had never been excited about going to work, but of course today was different. I would get to see a handsome man who I might be interested in. I rushed in and headed for the front office, and there he was, with his back turned, standing in the doorway of the office. I wasn't ready to face him just yet. Quickly, I made a detour to the nurse's office to spark up a good morning conversation with the school's nurse.

"Good morning, Nurse Clark. How are you doing this morning?"

"Good morning, Ms. Doxy. I'm good; wish the weekend was a little longer."

"Yeah, I know what you mean. I agree." *He should be gone now.* "Well, enjoy the rest of your day." Finally, he was gone. I signed in and hurried to my classroom.

"Good morning, Ms. Doxy," I heard a familiar voice say. *I know it's him oh my goodness, I hope my hair isn't out of place.* I turned around, and yes, it was he.

"Good morning," I said.

"So, who are you subbing for today?" he asked me. I was smiling from ear to ear. To my surprise, he didn't smile back. I felt those butterflies again.

"I'm subbing for...," I was too busy standing there in shock and trying to compose myself. I had had this vision before in a dream. I was at work talking to someone, but I couldn't see the person's face. It wasn't déjà vu.

This was real.

"Well, you have a good day," he said.

"You too," I ended, and he walked away.

I know he might think I'm crazy staring at him and looking like I just seen a ghost. Why didn't he smile? Do I have a booger in my nose or something? I rushed in the teacher's lounge to go to the bathroom. I looked in the mirror. *I look fine so what is his problem? Maybe he has a girlfriend. If so, why did he ask me to go to the movies? Whatever! Just like men they act like they are interested and end up having a wife or girlfriend. All men are dogs. I'm so sick of it. Wait, wait, and calm down, Jamila,* I stopped myself. *Okay, let's go back, think and review what happened at the movies the other night.*

After about three minutes of intense thinking, it dawned on me, *Oh, wow, I was a little distant that night. I wasn't there.* I mean, I was there physically, but my mind was somewhere else. My mind was so caught up in the fact that the two months of dreams that I had about six months ago was coming to reality. It seemed to be that every time I was in presence of him, I would remember a vision that I had about six months prior. *Now that is weird.* Finally, I gathered myself together and headed to my classroom.

I was an aide in a special education fifth grade classroom. Even though I fussed at them half the time, we shared a heart-warming relationship. They respected me because I disciplined them. I disciplined them out of love and they wanted that from me. They understood my feelings for them. I shared a piece of my heart with them every day. Don't get me wrong everyday was a challenge working with them, but it was worth it. I wouldn't change it for the world. They were all unique in their own special way. To be honest, I loved each and every one of them.

After an intense morning of introducing the students to a new lesson, I went to the teacher's lounge to take my fifteen-minute break. Still shocked by his coldshoulder attitude, I decided to text him to spark a conversation just to see where his mind was. I needed to know if he was still interested or if he had a change of heart. *Here goes nothing,* I said to myself as I pulled out my phone to break this weird barrier between the both of us.

"Hi, this is Ms. Doxy. How is your day going so far?" I waited for two minutes, then another two minutes. *Well, I guess he is busy. I'll try later on,* my mind convinced me. As I began to eat my snack, he walked in the teacher's lounge. "Hey, Ms. Doxy," he said. "Did you enjoy the movies last night?"

"Yes, I did. Did you?" I asked, throwing the ball back in his court. I added, "I just tried to text you."

"Oh, yeah?" he asked, acting like he was surprised that I had texted him. He pulled out his phone and smiled as he read the text. "I know I'm on my break," he said, "but I have some students in my room who I was having trouble with, so I have to go back to the classroom. You can join me if you want to."

"Well, I'm not on my lunch yet; I'm taking my fifteen-minute break right now. What time do you take your lunch break?"

"I take my lunch break at 1 p.m."

"Okay, my students have to go to music class, so I can come see you on your lunch," I responded, smiling.

"Okay," he said.

I couldn't stop smiling. As soon as he left the lounge, I got out my phone and began to text for the last five minutes I had on my break. There were some questions I needed to ask him. I needed to know if he was still interested or if this was just a thing to do because both of us were bored with life.

"Do you have any children?" While waiting for his response, I was thinking to myself that I hope he doesn't have two kids by two different baby mommas. It would be too much a headache for me, and I didn't have the patience for drama.

"I have two boys."

"Damn," I said out loud, not realizing I was speaking loudly; a co-worker looked over my way. Okay, I guess the fact that his boys had the same mother was better than them having different mothers.

"Do you have any children?" he texted back.

"Yes, I have a six-year-old son. Do you have your own house or apartment?" I responded.

"I live with my sister; and you?"

"I live with my mother."

"Tomorrow I am giving the students in my class a pizza party for good behavior. You are welcome to join us."

"I would love to. Just text me the time. I hate to cut this short, but I have to go back to the class. I go on my lunch break in another half an hour. You can meet me at Subway up the street," I texted him.

"Okay! :)" *Aw! He sent me a smiling face. Oh, my goodness, I feel like I'm back in high school again.* The butterflies in my stomach began to fly around in my stomach. After my fifteen-minute break was over, I headed back to the classroom. I entered the room with a smile. *I think he is still interested*, I said to myself.

Meanwhile, I couldn't stop looking at the clock. All of the sudden, time was slowed down. I glanced at the clock. *Can the time go any slower?* I thought to myself.

"Ms. Doxy, Ms. Doxy, Ms. Doxy!" one of the students interrupted my brief flashback.

"Yes?" I said in an irritated voice. I didn't want my daydream interrupted, but it was a good thing the student did interrupt me because I could have driven myself crazy by watching the clock like a hawk.

Finally, I was out of my daydreaming world and focused on my lesson with the students. Once I was engaged with the students, it was time for me to go to lunch. I hurried and gave the teacher the nod to let her know I was going on lunch. I grabbed my things and rushed out the door with a big Kool-Aid smile on my face. *Oh, Jamila, calm down. You are acting like a little high school girl. I'm sure he is not acting all excited and crazy as you are. Remember: he is the enemy. He is a man,* I thought to myself as I rushed to the car.

OUR LUNCH DATE

When I arrived at Subway, it was packed. *I'll never get to eat. Plus, I don't see his truck.* I walked in, and to my surprise there he was the second one in line with about eight people behind him. *Thank God.* Waving his hand so I could join him in line, I walked over and stood in front of him. I waited for someone to say something because I had gotten in front of him, but no one did.

"How did you get here so fast?" I asked him.

"I left a little early; you know, you don't have to call me "Mister," Ms. Doxy." *Oh, wow, he said that with authority in his voice. I like that.*

"I'm so used to calling you "Mister" at work; it's a habit."

"I know I was just kidding," he smiled. *Wow, he has a beautiful smile.*

I turned around and realized that I was the next person in line. I could actually feel him looking at me up and down. He was checking me out. I ordered my food and spotted a table where we could sit. While waiting for him to join me, I began to think about the men in my past. There were abusers. *I pray this man is not an abuser. Soul mate or not, I don't have the patience anymore to deal with drama. I just want to be happy. Doesn't everybody want to be happy?*

Finally, he sat down interrupting those mad-at-the world thoughts. When he sat down, he held both hands palms up and prayed over his food. *Oh, I like that too. That is a plus, a great sign. He acknowledges God. He might be a keeper. Some guys act like they are scared to mention God on a date.*

"So, you are a Muslim," I said.

"You can say that. I've been all my life."

"What mosque do you belong to?"

"Well, I don't go to the mosque anymore," he said.

"You eat Pork, I see."

"Well I believe that we can eat anything we want. I mean, being a Muslim is my foundation, but I believe there is good in every in religion."

"For me," I told him, "I had a solid background in Christianity, but I was introduced to Islam by my brother, and I had fallen in love with Islam, but now I don't believe in all that stuff."

"So, what do you believe?"

"I believe the same as you. I believe we are all one, and every religion is a reflection of God."

He smiled. "That's good we are on the same page,. Ms. Doxy" he said in a playful voice. His smile is priceless, I thought to myself.

"So, what are your hobbies? What do you like to do, Ms. Doxy?"

"I love to watch movies and enjoy my family. I just want to have fun!"

"I love to watch movies also. I always go to the theater downtown. Hey, if you are interested, I get free tickets to the screening of newly released movies, and you are welcome to join me."

"I would love to!" I said with this big Kool-Aid smile on my face. I couldn't help myself. I was into him and he was into me. It was the way we looked at each other. Little did he know, I knew about us before he did. I had many visions of us together on numerous occasions. *If he only knew that we were soul mates, maybe he will fall head over heels for me.* I didn't want him to think I was crazy or weird, so I kept that to myself.

"What is your passion?" I asked, to keep the flow of the conversation going.

"My passion is acting, and I like to write fiction also, but acting is my passion." "Really?" I responded.

"Yes. I want to be a famous actor someday; as a matter of fact, I've been in a couple of movies here in Chicago as an extra."

"Oh wow! What's an extra?"

"An extra is one of those people who you notice but you don't notice. They are the people that act as one of the people walking down the street, or the person who is in the restroom with the actor but doesn't have a speaking part."

"Do you get paid for it?"

"Of course, but it's not much. The people that usually do this kind of work don't do it for the check.

They have a passion for it like I do."

"Is this an all-day thing or a couple-of-hour's thing?"

"Well, we work the same hours as the main actors. It can be an all-day thing or an overnight thing. It mainly depends on how many times the director wants and can use you. Hey, if you want to, I'll take you on set as an extra so you can see for yourself what it's like for an extra on set."

"I think that will be fun. That will be great! I always wanted to know what it is like on a movie set." "What is your passion?" he returned the question.

"Well, that's a good question."

"Do you have a passion?" He looked at me with a concerned look.

"Yes, I have a passion; I just haven't being doing it. My passion is creative writing. I've been writing since the age of eleven. I used to write plays for my family Kwanzaa celebration." He looked impressed, which gave me the green light to continue to open up to him about the most important thing to me: my writing. "I have so many ideas for scripts," I went on, "but I never get to finish so I could publish or sell them. It's been a while since I've written anything."

"Why? It's your passion, right?"

"Yes, I always get discouraged, and I have listened to those dream-killers."

"Dream-killers?" he said with a puzzled look.

"Dream-killers are those who aren't capable of seeing the value of your dream so they discourage you out of fear for themselves. They don't mean any harm; it's just that they are ignorant to the fact of the reality of your dream. A dream-killer might be someone close to you. It could be your parents, a close friend, your sister or brother. Like I said, they don't mean you any harm, they just don't know the importance of your dream. Only you know how you feel about your dream." He was so intrigued with my response.

"You are a very intelligent woman."

I smiled. 'Thank you. You're not bad yourself." We both laughed. Not realizing how fast the time had gone, I glanced at the clock.

"Oh, wow, look at the clock," I said. He looked at the clock.

"Oh, wow! It's that late." We both gathered our things and rushed back to the school.

We couldn't stop smiling when we were in each other's company. At work, every time we saw each other in the hallway, we'd smile at each other. It didn't matter who was around. I felt like I was under a spell.

We had a great lunch. We seemed to have the important components that makes a healthy relationship last. As far as God goes, we were on the same page. Plus, he liked to write also. We had so much in common our belief in God was the same and we had similar passions. I had a great feeling about us. Like I said before, I had already seen us. We were happy, rich and we had children. I was so excited, but scared at the same time. I was happy and eager to see how all this was going to play out. I knew the result of us, but the key was getting to that designation of the relationship. This was only the second occasion we had the chance to really spend some time with each other, and I felt like I had known him for years. I was so excited about our development. The development between us from the "like" to "love" was the transition we were both waiting for. I knew it was the beginning of something beautiful, but I was also scared as hell. The fear of being hurt and betrayed was something I dreaded. I had been hurt and betrayed so many times, especially by my father. I guess that's what had begun my search for love.

BROKEN-HEARTED

A father's love is irreplaceable. It is so comforting. To experience a father's love teaches us how to love our heavenly father. I didn't know this, and at the time, I didn't really care for my father. I felt he betrayed me when he deserted me for this woman. What a smack in the face! Even though my mother and father had gotten a divorce, my father had still been active in my life until he met this woman. I remember the day he made the choice to remove himself from my life to please her insecure ways. I think that was one of the most hurtful experiences I had ever encountered.

The day of my high school graduation was one of the proudest and most rewarding days of my life. In a few hours I was going to be a proud graduate of Academy of Our Lady in Chicago, Illinois. Academy of Our Lady was an all-girls school. Unfortunately, it's a charter school now. However, one of my dreams is to reopen Academy of our Lady and turn it into a free magnet school for young women rich or poor.

Having the honor to attend this high school was a great experience. I was the one that chose to attend an all-girls school. I wanted to be able to express myself freely without having the fear of what the boys would think. I thought this decision I made for myself was wise and mature. I would not change anything about the four-year experience I had at Academy of Our Lady. It was a beautiful experience with my sisters. The bond that I had developed with them was wonderful. To this day, if I were to call and need one of my fellow alumnae sisters from the class of 1999, they would be there in my corner ready to support me.

As I was preparing myself to walk across the stage, I could hear my mother yelling in the next room. I rushed toward her room. She was on the phone, and, by the look on her face, I could tell she was talking with my father. She only has this look of disgust when she is talking to him.

"What's wrong, Mom?" I said eagerly, waiting for her to tell me who was on the other end of this phone dispute.

"I'm talking to your father."

"Well, what's the problem now?" I could feel my blood beginning to boil. I was getting agitated and pissed. This was a bad combination for me.

My mother had taken a minute to look at my face and she knew I was angry and hurt. When it came to my dad, it was always something with this woman. She didn't want me in the picture at all. If I wanted to spend time with my dad, she would make him feel guilty or threaten to leave him because she didn't want my mother around.

"Your father is considering not attending your high school graduation," she told me. "Jamila, go in the other room. Let me talk to your dad."

"No! Mom, let me talk to him. He needs to hear this from me."

She handed me the phone. "Dad," I said, "if you let another woman come between our relationship, then you don't deserve to be in my life." I gave my mom back the phone. She looked puzzled. She saw and heard in my voice how hurt I was. I walked out of the room. The anger inside wouldn't let me cry.

Emotionally, I had to gather myself because I was delivering a "Words of Wisdom" speech to the class of 1999. The anger had begun to roll off quickly and the excitement of graduating had taken over the thoughts of my passive father.

The graduation ceremony was beautiful. It was held in the back of the campus. It was so beautiful back there. There were flowers of every color. It was perfect. I nailed the speech perfectly. As I walked across the stage, I could feel a sense of freedom dwelling in me. I was so proud of myself as well as relieved. I glanced in the crowd to spot my mother, and to my surprise, there was my father. I didn't feel anything. Honestly, I didn't care whether he was there or not. Throughout the years of disappointments, I had become numb to any situation with my dad. For many years I have carried this pain. The pain of my father neglecting me to please his wife followed me. Little did I know, this was a stepping stone and a preparation of what God had planned for me.

THE SECRET'S OUT

The next morning as I was getting ready for work, all I could think about was going to see him. I couldn't wait to get there; plus, later I was meeting with Sarah the psychic. I remembered her saying, "I have to prepare something for you to give you the next time we meet." I couldn't wait until the day was over, but seeing him again added happiness to my day. Every time we passed each other in the hallway we would smile at each other and give each other compliments. There was no doubt in my mind that the spark was there. It was there and it was strong. I remember walking by the assistant principal's office and she called me in. She wanted to discuss something with me. Ms. Diane was really down-to-earth and sweet, and she kept the kids in check. She was a disciplinarian, like me.

"Ms. Doxy," she began, "I'm not trying to be in your business, but I must address this so we can keep it professional." She had serious look on her face. *What did these kids tell her now!* I thought to myself. She continued, "I've noticed something between you and him. I don't know if you are aware of it or not, but the students are paying close attention to you both."

"What do you mean paying close attention?"

"So, you really are not aware of it?" "Aware of what?" I asked with a curious look.

"The students are noticing the flirting between you and him."

"Oh, wow, I apologize. It's that noticeable?" I began to blush. "I didn't think they were paying attention, but I know better they pay attention to everything."

"I'm not trying to get in your business, but we can't let the students see it. We have to keep it professional."

"I understand, and you are right, but honesty, Ms. Diane, we didn't realize that we were being so open."

"Okay, now that we have gotten that out the way, are you guys really dating?" she said with an exciting voice. She had a big smile on her face. She seemed to be happy for us.

"Yes," I said immediately, with a smile on my face. "He is wonderful."

"Good, that's good," she responded. "I hate to cut this short but I have to get to this meeting."

"Oh, okay! Well, I want to thank you for bringing it to my attention. I wasn't aware of it.

"It's okay; we just have to realize that even when we aren't paying attention, they are always paying attention."

"You're right," I responded.

"I don't want to sound like I'm rushing but I have get to this meeting."

"Okay," I said and walked out of her office with a smile. I knew there was something special between us, but I didn't know other people could see it. I became more excited about the idea of him and me. We only had been dating for two weeks. *It's only been two weeks and I feel like we've been dating for about six months. This is really going fast,* I thought to myself as I walked back to the classroom to escort the students to gym. Today the time was flying. It was twelve o'clock and only three more hours until I could go see Sarah. I was excited and curious as to what she had to give to me.

On my break, I texted him what had happened in Ms. Diane's office. He felt bad because he was worried I would lose my job.

"Don't be sorry. Trust me: I'm not going to lose my job. They need me!"

"Well, maybe I can just sub at the other two schools instead of this one since you are here, because I can't help these feelings that I am developing for you. Whatever this thing is that is growing between us is happening fast. The crazy thing about it is that I'm trying to control my feelings for you. I don't want you to feel I'm moving too fast, but I can't help it. I feel like I'm under a spell."

I read his text with a big smile on my face. I was blushing like crazy. I texted back, "No don't try to avoid me. We just have to be professional when we are around the students, that's all, but I also feel the same way. I am developing feelings for you really fast. It's only been two weeks and my feeling is strong. I can't stop smiling when I see you. I try to control it, but it's like I'm not in control. So don't try to avoid me because I'm going to think you aren't interested anymore. LOL."

He texted back, "No, I don't want you to ever think I'm avoiding you. I like seeing your beautiful face; I just don't want you to get in any trouble, but I can't control my feelings for you. The students are back, so I will text you on my break.

"Okay," I responded.

I wanted to text him and tell him that we are going to fall deeply in love. I'd had a vision of us living together and being with each other. Since I'd been in contact with him, I'd been having these dreams about our future. There was one dream where we were riding in a truck and he was talking and I was looking at him smiling, and then there was this one dream that was so vivid. It kept coming to the surface of my mind. I know this might sound a little crazy, but before I had known him in person I dreamed about him, but I couldn't see the face. I had dreamt about him six months prior. In the dream, he and I were dressed up in formal clothing and he was speaking to a group of people, but this place was big and there were people everywhere. We were so happy, and by the way we were dressed, it seemed to me that we were rich. Most importantly, we were at peace with our lives together. I wanted to tell him so badly about this dream, but I didn't want him to think that I was crazy. I had made up my mind to tell him when the time was right.

    I hurried back to the class for the last hour. That last hour was intense. I couldn't wait to tell Sarah the psychic what had happened so far between him and me. My soul mate and I were hitting it off pretty well indeed. I couldn't stop smiling. I didn't let anyone or anything take away my feelings of happiness I was having. The feeling of being in bliss is real. For so long I never understood when people use to refer to love as bliss. I wanted to make sure I was in bliss and not in lust. I knew I was attracted to him but I never looked at him in a way that I wanted to have sex with him. I knew it wasn't lust. It couldn't be because the feelings that I had for him were of love not lust.

    The bell rang and it was dismissal time. "Yes," I said to myself as I prepared to do hallway duty. The thoughts of fear began to pour into my mind. *He might be just pretending with me. He is an actor. He has expertise in pretending.* I was getting pissed because all of those memories of my past relationship had begun to play out in my mind. *What makes him so different from the other men who abused or betrayed me?* Suddenly, those negative thoughts vanished when I saw him walk past me. We both tried to hold in our smiles but it didn't work. The smiles won over and we had exchanged our last flirtatious smiles for the day. He was off to another school to work for an after-school program. I knew he would be calling me in about fifteen minutes. After my duty was over, I rushed back to the classroom to get my phone and just as I was pulling out my phone to call him when suddenly he called my phone.

"Hey, as I was calling you, the phone rang and it was you. What a coincidence!" I told him.

"We've been having a lot of coincidences between us lately. Well, I'm off to this other job. I just wanted to hear your voice before I got on the expressway."

"Oh, that's sweet of you." I couldn't stop smiling. "Well, you enjoy the rest of your day and give me a call when you are done."

"What are you about to do?"

"I'm about to write up these referrals for some students; then I'm going to head home."

"Don't you have to pick up your son?"

"Well, my mother picks him up for me." "Oh, well, I'll talk to you soon."

"Okay, bye," I said, but there was a silence on the phone. Neither one of us wanted to get off the phone.

"Hang up!" he said.

"You hang up!" I said laughing. We both were laughing. "This is so cute, we don't want to get off the phone."

"I know it is cute. Okay, on the count of three, we both hang up. Okay!"

"Okay." We both began to count one...two...three. There was a silence again. Realizing that neither one of us had hung up the phone, we began to laugh again.

"This is crazy," he said.

"I know, right? Okay, for real I have to go and I don't want you to have an accident while talking and driving, so I will talk to you later. Bye." I didn't want to hang up, but

I had to hurry and write the referrals so I could go meet Sarah. I didn't discuss with him the part where I going to see Sarah because the thought of me going to talk with a psychic might scare him off. God knows I didn't want to do that. Things were going great and I didn't want anything to come between us.

THE MEETING

I pulled up to Sarah's house with excitement. I wonder if I could sense when I pull up. What does she see? I thought to myself. As I walked in Sarah's small cozy home, I felt so comfortable. It seemed like I'd known her for a while. Our friendship was blossoming. Even though it had only been a week since we've known each other, we had been keeping in touch over the phone. I would call her and discuss whatever on my mind. Don't get me wrong there were times when I had to ask myself how I could be so comfortable with someone I have known for such a short time, but the bond between her and me was irresistible. I knew there was something more than what she was telling me. I felt like I was becoming a part of a secret society.

"So, Jamila, you have a lot to tell me. How was the date?" she asked me. I was so excited, I felt like a high school girl blabbering about her first date.

"It was great. He is such a wonderful person." "So, both of you work at the same school?" she said. "Yes, which is a plus because I get to see him just about every day."

"That's great, Jamila! So, how have you been feeling?"

"I'm good," I said, a little confused as to why she had asked that.

"I mean, how you feel physically?" she asked.

"Are you in any pain?"

"I have experienced pain for many years now; I've just learned to deal with it," I replied.

"Jamila, that is not the way God wants you to live your life. He doesn't want us to be in pain all the time." I looked at her like she was crazy because no one had ever told me this.

"Well I have had endometriosis for a long time and it flares up every once and a while so I do I get rid of that pain."

"The pain I'm talking about is the pain you wake up with every morning. It feels like you've been hit by a truck."

"You are right." I stared at her with a curious look. *How did she know about that?* I asked myself quietly. She pulled out a plastic bag with some soap in it.

"This is what I've been preparing for you. I want you to wash up with this soap every day for seven days. This soap will cleanse you of that man who you were with before your soul mate who you are currently dating now. It will also get rid of that pain you've been waking up with for years. Girl, this soap will make you light as a feather." I put the soap in my purse. "Remember: do not use anything else on your body. Use only the soap."

I nodded, but I was disappointed. *I was expecting some magic potion or something. I mean she is a psychic right, so where is the real magic. Soap? Are you serious?* There was silence for about ten seconds.

"So, are you guys going to see each other again?" she asked to kill the silence. "Yes, we are."

"You are very blessed to have met your soul mate, Jamila. You should be excited!"

"I am very thankful. I feel like we've known each other for ages. He has a beautiful smile as well as personality."

"He is just like you. He is your soul mate!" I smiled and blushed a little. By the look on her face, I could tell she was withholding more information. We talked about him and me for about ten minutes, thinking about some more intimate date ideas that we could engage in.

"I want you to come back and see me after you have used the soap for seven days. In the meantime, girl, keep me informed about how you and your soul mate are doing. Girl, it's exciting to be with your soul mate. You should be happy. If you want to talk about anything, don't hesitant to call me. If I don't answer the phone; I'm usually with a client; just leave a message and I will call you back as soon as possible."

LOVE AT FIRST SIGHT

I was shocked that the visit was so short. I was only there for about twenty-five minutes. I was expecting her to tell me more, much more! But I was tired and eager to get home to my son so I didn't mind. Plus, I wanted to try out this so-called "magical soap." When I had gotten home, Jalon was watching television with my mother. We ate dinner together and Jalon and I popped some popcorn and watched a movie.

RING, RING! I jumped out of bed to look for my phone. I knew it was him. *Why is it every time I need this phone, I can never find it?! Are you serious? Where is it? Maybe I need to tape the phone to my forehead.* I was running around the room like a mad woman. Jalon was laughing at me. His joyous laugh was keeping me from having a fit.

"Mom, Mom!"

"Not now, Jalon. I'm trying to find this phone."

"But Mom!"

"Boy, didn't I tell you 'Not right now'?" I turned around and there was Jalon waving my phone in the air smiling.

"It's been in the bed for the longest time, Mom. I tried to tell you." I couldn't do anything but laugh. We both began to laugh together.

"Thank you, baby," I kissed and hugged him.

"What would I do without you?"

As I looked at the phone, I saw a missed call from him. *Okay, Jamila, don't call him right back; wait for about thirty minutes. You don't want to look like you're desperate,* I said to myself. I tried to wait but I couldn't.

"Hello?" he answered.

"Hey, how was work?" I said.

"It was okay. All I could think about was you."

I was blushing from head to toe. "Aw, that's so sweet."

"No, for real this has never happened this fast for me before. I couldn't really focus at work because I was thinking about us."

"What about us?" I replied with a curiosity.

"Is this really 'love at first sight'? Is this really possible? I was asking myself this question over and over. When I had gotten home, I asked my mom if she believes in 'love at first sight.'"

"What did she say?"

"She said 'yes.' She said that's true love." I felt a chill run through my body. "Do you believe in 'love at first sight'?" he asked me.

"Honesty and truly, I use to mock the idea of having love for someone at first sight. I've never experienced anything like this before, and I really think whatever this is between us is going to grow into something beautiful.

Do you believe in having a soul mate?" "Yes, I do," he replied.

"I feel many people mistake lust for love, and they think that it is 'love at first sight' but it's really 'lust at first sight.' But I haven't looked at you in that way. When I met you, I felt a connection. From my understanding of things when a person meets their soul mate, the love connection goes quickly because the souls have already met, so it doesn't take long for the love to develop between the two people."

"Do you think we are soul mates?" he asked.

"Yes, I do. Definitely." There was a minute of silence on the phone. "Well what's on your agenda tomorrow?" I asked, to break the weird silence between us.

"Same thing tomorrow. Hopefully, the school will call me in to sub."

"I hope so; I would love to see your face again." Although I couldn't see him, by the way he laughed I could tell he was smiling.

"I'm going to call you before I go to bed. I need to fix me something to eat. I'm starving."

"Okay, just call me later then."

"Bye." As usual I didn't want to get off the phone with him. We had a connection that was unexplainable. I guess 'love at first sight' is true after all. To my surprise I looked over to see Jalon sleeping so peacefully. I didn't want to wake him up, so I decided to join him for a quick hour nap. I lay down and as soon as I got comfortable, I passed out.

◆

She can't move, and every time she tries, the straps seem to squeeze her wrists tighter. The voice in her head is getting louder and louder. She screams and screams. Fear is all around her, but she can't escape the chokehold that the negative spirits have on her. She cries and screams until she is exhausted, but feels a sense of comfort. A feeling of relief surrounds her now. Just as she becomes calm, the voice in her head starts again, and she can feel all the hurt that she was a victim of and all the hurt that she caused. The feeling is unbearable but the strength within keeps her fighting for control of her mind.

She tries to figure out what is going on but her intellect is hindered by the voice in her head.

◆

I awoke in a sweat. *Why did I dream about some woman being in a mental institution? Maybe this is an idea of a script. I can use this part with the other scripts I had begun to write,* I thought to myself. I changed my clothes and woke up Jalon so he could change into his night clothes. The hour nap turned into a three-hour nap. I felt well rested, but eager to finish the dream. I went back to sleep thinking I was going to finish the dream, but I guess I was more tired than I realized.

The next day I woke up and hurried to take my shower. I wanted to see if this 'magical soap' that Sarah had given me would work. Believe it or not, after using the soap I felt a little lighter. Some of the heaviness was lifted off me. "Wow, this stuff really works," I said to myself. To my surprise, I had more energy than I usually have, and I went off to work. My mornings were pretty much the same every day except for the growing feeling I was developing for him. The feelings I had for him were intense. There were nights when we would talk on the phone holding conversations about past relationships and things that related to a maintaining a healthy relationship. Next weekend was Halloween and we were planning to introduce our boys to each other. He had twins who I was eager to meet, and he wanted to meet my pride and joy Jalon. Every year, the town I lived in has a weekend full of activities so we decided to spend that Friday getting involved in the activities in my hometown. Then on Saturday, Jalon and I would meet him and his family at his house.

HALLOWEEN BASH

Halloween arrived and we attended the Friday festivities. The boys hit it off really well. They played well together. As we were engaged in decorating our pumpkins, I had a strong sense of déjà vu. It was so clear. I had dreamed this moment and time with him. I stopped and paused for about a minute.

"Hey, are you okay?" He asked. There were times I wanted to tell him how we were meant to be with each other. I wanted to tell him that I had seen our future together. In my mind I was so excited about our future that I wanted to speed things up. I wanted us to hurry up get married and have these six kids we were going to have. In the vision I dreamed about, our success and love was amazing. Well, maybe if we could only get into the financial success first. My mind was going and going.

"Hey, I said are you okay?"

"I'm fine."

"What were you thinking about?"

"What do you mean?"

"It looked like you were in deep thought about something."

"Oh, it wasn't anything," I said, trying to buy a little time while I thought about a response. *I'm just going to tell him the truth*, I thought to myself.

"Come on now, we are better than that. You can tell me anything." He was always sincere about my feelings. He was also a great listener. Whenever I thought he wasn't paying attention to me, he could always tell me word for word what I had said. I've never had a man who was interested in listening to what I had to say.

"If things work out between us, I was imaging how our life together would be."

"Our life would be perfect together," he said with confidence. I smiled as I continued to decorate my small pumpkin. At that moment I was so happy to be in the company of this man. Everything about him seemed to be perfect. He was intelligent, handsome, family- and goal oriented, God-fearing, and let's not forget he was tall. I never really dated tall men but I've always thought that they were sexy. He was all the above. He was perfect in my eyes.

The evening had come to a closure and Jalon and the boys had gotten along well with each other. As I drove home, all I could think about was meeting his family tomorrow. Tomorrow was Halloween and we were taking the kids treat-or-treating around his house in the City. I was excited and nervous at the same time.

"Mom, are we going to see them again?" Jalon asked.

"Yes honey, we are going over to their house tomorrow for trick-or-treating." "YES!" he said.

RING, RING! A smile appeared on my face because I knew it was him.

"Hello?"

"I miss you," he said, and I felt chill run through my body.

"I miss you, too."

"You know what I was thinking? I'm going to think of nickname to call you, and I have one in mind." "What is it?" I asked.

"Naw, you might think it's corny."

"No, I won't. Come on; tell me," I prodded.

"Sunshine. That's the name I had in mind for you. You bring so much happiness and light to my life."

"Aw, I love that name. I think it fits me well."

"Now I have to think of a nickname for you. Well, I'm at home, so call or text me when you get home."

"Okay, bye." As I looked in the backseat, Jalon was sound asleep. I carried him into the house to his bed. It's amazing and touches my heart to see the peace and love that Jalon brings to my heart when he is sleeping. It's something about the peaceful look a child has when he or she is sleeping. The innocence of a child becomes more valuable in the eyes of the parent.

RING, RING!

"Hello?"

"Yeah, I just made it home. The boys are knocked out."

"Same here with Jalon. He is so excited about tomorrow. He really enjoyed himself tonight.'"

"The boys asked about him also. So what time are you and Jalon coming over?"

"What time do you want to me to be there?'

"It's up to you. I don't know what's on your schedule."

"You are on my schedule. I have nothing on my schedule. The only thing that I have to do on my schedule is you;"

"Oh, yeah, you sure about that?" he joked.

"Yes, I'm sure." I wanted our relationship to go to the next level. "There is something I need to ask you before I ask you the second thing I need to ask you."

"Okay, tell me, what is it?"

"Are we officially together as a couple, or are we still dating?" He paused for a couple of seconds. "I mean, be honest with me; if you think we are moving too fast, let me know."

"Yes, I feel we are moving fast, but I think this is something neither one of us has control of. I feel we are a couple dating and getting to know each other."

"I feel the same."

"So, what's the other question?" he asked. I thought he had forgotten about the second question.

"Oh, never mind."

"No, tell me."

"Okay. My body is telling me it's time to make love, but my heart is telling me to wait until we both say and mean those powerful words: 'I love you.'"

"I've been feeling the same way, and I agree. I think we should wait until we love each other. Oh wow!"

"What?"

"Now you have me visualizing how it would be with you. Please change the subject."

"Okay, I'm exhausted, so I'm going to call it a night. We will be there at 3 p.m. Is that okay?"

"Yeah, that's cool. Bye, my sunshine." I couldn't stop blushing and giggling.

"Bye, my prince. Your nickname is my prince. You are my Prince Charming, so loving and sweet."

"Aw," he said. "Okay, see you tomorrow."

A part of him never wanted to get off the phone. We both cherished every conversation on the phone. Whether it lasted two minutes or two hours, hearing each other's voice had given us a sense of comfort.

"Okay, bye," I said.

THE PARENT'S INTRODUCTION

The day of Halloween was exciting for Jalon and me. Jalon had awakened me at 7:00 in the morning. I had to convince him to go back to asleep, but I wasn't too convincing. He kept asking for the boys. When he found out that we wouldn't be able to see them until 3:00 p.m., he became restless.

"But Mom, that's too long. Why do I have to wait so long to see the boys?" Jalon said.

"Jalon, we don't know what they have to do." "Mom, did you call him?

"No, I didn't, and I'm not going to. We are going later and that's final."

RING, RING! Of course, I had to search around to find the phone again.

"Here, Mom; it's him." Holding my phone in his hand, he could not stop jumping for excitement. I've never seen him so excited about seeing people before.

"Thank you, Jalon," I said to him, and then he gave me the phone. "Hello?"

"Good morning, sunshine."

"Good morning, my prince."

"You should see my son right now. He is so excited. He can't stop jumping up and down. He can't wait until 3:00 to see all of you. I told him that I didn't know what y'all had to do"

"I'm with Jalon. I can't wait 'til 3:00 to see you either. If it's okay with your mom, could we come over and visit?"

"I think that will be a great idea; plus, you can meet my mother. Did you guys eat breakfast yet?"

"No, I just woke up with you on my mind."

"Aw, that's so sweet. It's almost 8:30. Why don't y'all come over now and I will fix all of us breakfast."

"You will do that?"

"Yes. It's no problem."

"Do you need me to bring anything?" he asked.

"Could you bring a carton of eggs to replace the eggs the ones I'm about to use to make our gourmet breakfast?"

"So, can you throw down, huh?"

"Most definitely, your girl doesn't play any games when it comes to food."

"The boys and I will be there in an hour."

"Okay, bye."

"Bye." I hung up the phone in a hurry and rushed to my closet to find something to wear. I didn't have much time to find something to wear, realizing I only had an hour to get dressed.

"Mom, so what did he say?" "They are on their way, Jalon." "Yes!" he said.

"Go straighten up your room." To my surprise, Jalon was excited just as I was. I've never seen him so eager to clean his room. I changed clothes at least five times. Finally, after spending almost thirty minutes trying on clothes, I found this white button-up and a pair of dark denim jeans. Breakfast was ready just in time before they arrived.

I introduced him and the boys to my mother.

"Good morning, Mrs. Doxy." He tried to give an introductory handshake, but my mother being the perfect and beautiful soul that God created her to be, she held her arms open.

"Now you give me a hug," she said. I could see he was shocked at my mother's friendly way of greeting. She hugged the boys also.

"So, what's on the menu, Jamila?" he asked.

"Well, we have turkey bacon, sausages, scrambled cheese eggs, pancakes, and grits."

"This is a lot of food. Are you expecting anyone else to come over?"

"No, that's how I cook. I usually cook more than I expect to cook." We all sat down as a family and ate breakfast. Sitting there eating as a family reminded me how important family is. Since I was a young child, all I ever wanted was to be a successful writer and have a big family. Family comes first in my eyes. I felt like we'd been a family for many years. It felt so right.

I gave them a brief tour of our home. Jalon and the boys began to play in his room. I showed him my room.

"And this is where I get my beauty rest at." He walked behind me, and as I turned around he kissed me and we began to kiss each other. His lips were soft as feathers. I could feel my body temperature rising as we continued to kiss. I pushed him on the bed and sat in his lap. The more I kissed him the more curious I had gotten to know what it would be like to be intimate with each other. Whispering in his ear some enticing words, we continued to kiss.

"Stop!" I jumped up. "I'm sorry. I don't want to lead you on. For a minute I had forgotten where we were.

Plus, we said we were going to wait," I said, trying to control my hormones.

"Don't apologize. I feel we shouldn't put a time on it. When it happens, it will happen. Plus, we are only kissing, Jamila.

"You are right! But the kids are in the next room."

We both looked at each in a way that said we should stop before the kissing leads to further interaction. We walked out of my room to the living room. I turned on the television. We couldn't stop blushing at each other. We didn't watch the television. We began to talk. We talked for at least two hours. Finally realizing it was only 11 a.m., I suggested that we take the kids to McDonald's Playland for a couple of hours. The boys were so excited to be in each other's company. We talked and talked. We talked about past relationships as well as future outings that we wanted to take the boys on.

He was my dreaming 'Prince Charming' and I was his 'Sunshine' and little did he know, I knew how all this was going to turn out. I couldn't wait until we got to that point. The point of true love and financial success was where we were headed.

If only I could've sped up time. Before we knew it, it was time to head to his parents' home. I was a little nervous about meeting his parents after only two weeks of dating, but it wasn't like we were telling them we were getting married or anything. I considered myself to be a good woman. *There isn't anyone like Jamila.* I was prepping myself to meet his parents as I followed him in my car to his parents' home. When I met his parents, I didn't want to appear so nervous or unsure of myself, so giving me a pep talk wasn't a bad idea. Jalon rode with him and the boys so I didn't feel weird about talking to myself.

As we pulled up in front of this big bungalow home, my heart began to race and my mouth became dry. "Oh, my God, this is the house I dreamed about," I said out loud while I parked the car. Every time I was in the company of him, the series of dreams that I had dreamed about in March which was eight months prior was becoming a reality. There was one thought that stayed swarming in my mind and that was *WHY*. I sat there in shock, trying to recall the dream I had had eight months before. It seemed the only time I remembered the vision was when I was in the present time, and then it would trigger the remembrance of the events of the dream. This was getting more interesting by the day.

The sound of him knocking on the window startled me and interfered my daydreaming. I wanted to know so badly what the purpose of all this was. *Why were we destined to meet?*

"Are you okay?"

"Yeah, I'm okay," I said as I exhaled and opened the door.

"It looks like you've seen a ghost. Are you sure you okay?"

"Yeah, I'm fine."

As I entered the home, I looked to the right and saw it. I saw a sword at the top of the mantle. There was a sword, a picture of Elijah Muhammad, and the Quran. The visions I dreamed were right. In my vision I kept seeing these same items on top of a mantle. Six months ago I didn't have a clue of the purpose of these visions, but now it was beginning to make sense. Sitting on his couch while Jalon and I waited to see his parents, I tried to put the pieces together, but I was still in shock of what was happening. I had dreamed my future. I mean, I used to have déjà vu but not to this extent. What was happening to me wasn't normal and I needed to talk to Sarah. *She would know*, I thought to myself. As soon as I heard the door open across from where Jalon and I were sitting, I stood up and his parents walked out of the room. His mother was tall, of brown-complexion, and had a beautiful smile. She seemed to be down-to-earth and fun.

His father was short, of light-complexion, and seemed to be the serious one.

He introduced me to his parents. As I reached out my hand to give them an introductory handshake, I could feel my leg begin to shake. I was so nervous.

"My name is Jamila, and this is my six-year-old son Jalon."

"I heard so many good things about you," his mother said. I began to blush, and the nervousness eventually left.

"I hope there were good things he said about me," I said, and we both smiled and laughed.

"Of course they were," she responded.

WILL AND JADA SMITH WANNABES

He had taken the boys upstairs to get dressed for treat-or-treating. I had my costume in my bag and changed in the bathroom. I was dressed as the character Trinity from the movie The Matrix. I wanted to surprise everyone. I could hear them coming down the stairs. "Mom, are you dressing up too?" Jalon said.

"Yeah do you like it?"

"Yeah, Mom, I really like it."

"So, can you tell me who Jamila is dressed as?" he said with a big smile on his face.

"She is Super Woman," one of the boys shouted. They guessed for a good two minutes.

"Do you know who I am?" I said with a flirtatious smile looking into his eyes.

"Of course, you are Jada Pinkett Smith in the movie *Matrix 3*."

"You are close but I was thinking about Trinity."

"But you look more like Jada Pinkett Smith," he said returning the flirtatious smile.

"Okay, well Jada it is," I said. We all had gone outside so his mother could take pictures.

"I thought you said you were going to dress up, so I won't be the only overgrown person dressed up," I whispered to him while we were posing for the pictures.

"I didn't have enough money to buy a costume. I was going to tell you but it slipped my mind. Are you mad?"

"Why would I be mad? I understand!"

"I have to use the bathroom. I'll be right back." They played in the front yard while I sat on the porch enjoying the wonderful weather. It wasn't cold at all. It was close to fifty-five degrees that day and the sun was shining bright. All of a sudden the boys stopped in their tracks and looked at me with a strange look on their faces. I looked down at my chest to see if I had drooled on myself or something.

"What's wrong you guys?" I asked. Instead of answering they pointed at me and I turned around to see what were they looking at, and I jumped and screamed when I saw it. I almost fell down the stairs but he caught me just in time. He was dressed as the clown in the movie *Saw*.

"You scared the crap out of me," I whispered to him. "I wanted to surprise you. Do you like it?"

"I think it is very cool. Where did you get the costume? It looks so real."

"I brought the mask off this costume website."

"I really like it."

"Well, let us begin our journey before it gets too dark." As the boys went door to door treat-or-treating, we walked behind them holding hands and periodically giving each other smiles. At that moment being there with him, I felt like I was floating on clouds. We stopped a couple of times and he introduced me to some of his childhood friends. One of his friends said that we reminded him of Will and Jada Smith. I was dressed up as her, and when he took off the mask he only had a suit on. Plus, he is tall and handsome like Will Smith, but, *my boo looks better than Will,* I thought to myself.

"Y'all look like y'all are on a mission, like y'all are about to conquer the world or something," one of his friends said. I wanted to comment so badly. I wanted to say, "Yes, we will conquer the world together, and I've seen it." Of course, I kept the comment to myself. Meanwhile, the boys were having a ball. They enjoyed each other's company and gathered an enormous amount of candy in such little time. We only trick-or-treated for about forty-five minutes and the boys' bags were almost full. However, we were so caught up in the moment of being with each other that we had forgotten how long we were out.

"Wow, look at the time. It's six o'clock already.

It's been three hours."

"Yeah, look at the time; are you trying to leave me?" he slightly squeezed my hand and gave me a look to let me know he was cherishing the moment and he didn't want to let me go. The day had turned out to be a beautiful night. I also didn't want the night to end, but I knew the day would come when we would wake up to each other smiling, and of course I look forward to the morning breath.

"I'm really enjoying our time together and since I don't want to let you go either, I'm going to stick around for another hour."

"Good, I can pop some popcorn, and me, you, and the boys can watch some Avatar episodes," he said convincingly.

"That sound great to me," I said. We hurried in to sit back and relax. I was exhausted. We had been walking for three hours; plus, having the disturbing dream the previous night and the fact that Jalon had awaken me at 7 a.m. didn't help either. Even though my eyes were fixed on the television, my mind was somewhere else. I couldn't wait to call Sarah in the morning. Plus, the time was overdue for Sarah and me to meet. I was to meet with her again after using the soap. It had been two weeks. Then I realized that the next day was Sunday, I had planned to call and leave her a message and wait until she returned my call but I was sure she would be in church all day.

It seemed to me every time I was with him enjoying myself the time went by so quickly. Jalon dreaded to leave the boys. I didn't look forward to this thirty to thirty-five minute drive home, but it was time for Jalon and me to depart from him and the boys. Jalon and I said our good-byes and left. During the long ride home all I could think about was meeting with Sarah. I had many questions that needed answers, like "Why am I having so many premonitions of my time with this man?" Finally, we arrived home. Jalon and I rushed in the bed. I texted him that I was home and nearly passed out into a deep sleep.

PSYCHIC TALK

Sunday morning Jalon and I slept in until 11:00 a.m. I was surprised my mother didn't come in and hassle me about going to church. Instead she let us sleep peacefully. I mean, church wasn't my thing. I'd never caught the Holy Ghost and didn't want to. I had heard too many stories about ministers sleeping with the women of the church. In my eyes there were too many hypocrites in Christianity as well as Islam. I had good knowledge of both of them, but to be honest, I was confused as hell.

RING, RING! I had a feeling it was Sarah who was calling. I had left her numerous messages saying I needed to talk with her as soon as possible. Instead, it was him.

"Good morning, sunshine," he said.

"Good morning," I responded with irritation in my voice.

"What's wrong?"

"There nothing wrong."

"Yes, there is. I can hear it in your voice."

I wasn't ready to tell him about me going to see a psychic. "Oh, just something I was dealing with here."

"Do you want to talk about it?" he asked with sincerity.

"No, I'm okay. I have something to ask you." Changing the subject fast was my motive. I didn't want to continue to lie to him.

"What is it? You can ask me anything." "Have you ever had a reading by a psychic?' "No! Have you?" he asked.

"Yes, I did the other day. Hey, I got an idea why don't you go get a reading and we can compare our readings."

"Jamila, I don't believe in that stuff. Psychics are scam artists who take people's money."

"Come on! Do it for me." I wanted him to get a reading by Sarah because I knew he would ask questions about me and maybe she will tell him the truth about us. She would tell him how we are soul mates and anything else about our future.

"Okay, Jamila, I'm only doing this for you." "Okay," I said with a smile on my face.

"So, what are you doing today?" he asked.

"Nothing much, I'm going to do a little cleaning and then Jalon and I might go to the movies in a couple of hours."

"Is it possible for me to come see you today? I really want to see you."

"Aw, that's so sweet. Of course you can. Do you want to meet us at the movie theater around 3:30? I'm on the internet now checking out the movie times."

"I was hoping I could come see you now!"

"Well, I have to discuss that with my mother first, so I'm going to call you back in about fifteen minutes."

"Okay," he said. I hung up the phone and skipped to my mother's room in excitement.

I informed my mother that he was coming over so he could go to the movies with Jalon and me. Of course, she had become concerned knowing we had begun to spend most of our time together.

"Don't you think you moving too fast? You've been through a lot with the men in your past, and it wasn't that long ago," she said.

"I know, I know, but it's different with him. He is so wonderful, Mom. We have so much in common. Plus, it not like I'm trying to marry the man, Mom."

"Okay, Jamila, I just don't want you to get hurt."

"Oh, Mom, you know I can handle it."

"Well, I don't have any problem with him coming over." I grabbed my phone and informed him he could come over. I was so thrilled to know I was going to see him again, and then another call was coming through. It was Sarah.

"Hi, Jamila, I got your messages. Is everything okay?"

"I wanted us to meet because I have some questions that I need answers too, but first he wants to come in to get a reading."

"Okay that's fine. What day does he want to come?"

"Well, if he is called in to work, I will call you on my lunch to confirm, so let's schedule for tomorrow."

"That's fine, Jamila. I hope to see him soon,. Bye."

"All right, bye." I hung up the phone feeling so excited because finally Sarah would get a chance to tell him about me. *I know he is going to ask her about me and I don't have to walk around feeling weird and out of place when I'm around him,* I thought to myself.

RING, RING! I had forgotten that he was on the other end.

"Hello, what happened, Jamila?"

"I'm so sorry, but that was Sarah the psychic. I made an appointment for you tomorrow after work."

"If I work. Jamila, I didn't know you were into this psychic stuff so deep." I could tell he was getting concerned about me seeing a psychic.

"Well, I'm not deep into it. I'm just a little curious." On the inside I wanted to tell him that I dreamed about our future together and we were living it out right now. *He might think I am crazy if I tell him that. I'll wait until Sarah talks to him,* I thought to myself.

"So, how many times do you talk to this psychic?"

"Her name is Sarah, and she is not just a psychic; she has become a good friend. I don't see her that much, but we talk on the phone a lot. Why did you ask?" By the sound of my voice, he knew I was getting irritated and he changed the subject. In my mind Sarah was the only one who understood my uniqueness. I was lost and confused and I felt Sarah was sent by God to help me.

"Well, can I still come over to you? I really want to see you," he said, interrupting the flow of my thoughts. "That's fine," I said.

"I'll be there in an hour."

"Okay, I'll see you when you get here. I can't wait to see you."

"I can't wait to see you, too. Bye".

"Bye."

An hour hadn't passed yet and I heard a knock on the door. I opened the door and it was he.

"How you get here so fast?"

"I was already en route when I was talking to you." He kissed me at the door and gave me a tight hug. I didn't want to let go, but I could hear my nosey son Jalon walking toward the door and I had to let go.

"Hey!" Jalon said. "Where are the boys?"

"They are with their mother."

"Why didn't you bring them with you?" Jalon said with concern.

"Jalon, stop with all the questions. Go straighten up your room while we talk." As soon as Jalon walked to the back, he gently grabbed me and kissed me. I'm not trying to be corny or anything, but that kiss made me feel like I was floating. I felt like I was under a spell when he was around. I couldn't get the fact out of my mind that it had only been two weeks since we've been dating.

"I'm sorry for being so forward, but I can't help myself. What is this between us? I've never felt this way about someone so soon." As we hugged each other close resting in each other arms, I could hear his heartbeat. I thought to myself, *Wow, this is real. This is what true love feels like.*

Although the movie didn't start for another two hours, being in each other's company fed the hunger inside. It was the craving to feel, hear, and touch each other. Whether we were engaged in a conversation, or sitting next to each other holding hands, we were content with each other. We were in bliss.

THE BIG DAY

I woke up with a smile on my face. I enjoyed the time I had spent with him. It felt wonderful to go to the movies as a family. Also, it was the day he goes to see Sarah for a reading. I couldn't wait. I was more excited than he was considering that he didn't believe in the "psychic stuff." Maybe he would understand what I'd been going through with the visions of the future. I felt that something good would come out of it. I was so glad that he was called into work so I could see his face, and of course I had to call Sarah to confirm his appointment. The day at work was like any other day. The time dragged as usual, but he and I made sure we exchanged flirtatious smiles throughout the day.

Finally, the day of work had come to an end. The plan was for him to go see Sarah while I went home and waited impatiently for him to call. He was to meet me at my house after his appointment. To keep my mind off of things, I did the usual: helped Jalon with his homework, then I began to do little cleaning. Unfortunately, it didn't help. I wanted to know so badly what they were talking about.

Knock, Knock. Someone was at the door and I knew it wasn't him. It'd only had been about twenty minutes since I had talked to him. But I was wrong it was him.

"So, what did she say?" I didn't give him a chance to speak or step in the house good. "Let's go to my room so you can tell me what happened." I grabbed his hand and rushed to my room and closed the door. "So, what happened, honey? What did she tell you?"

"She told me many things about myself."

"Did she say anything about us?" I wasn't really interested in what she said about him personally. I was too focused on us.

"She did say that we were soul mates and that my writing will be successful."

"What else did she say?"

"I see you are so taken by what this woman tells you. When you go see her do you have to pay all the time?" Right away, my whole demeanor changed from excitement to defensive. I knew what he was trying to get at. Since he didn't believe, I knew he wouldn't understand what I thought he was ready to hear. I wanted to tell him but he wasn't ready to hear about the visions of our future. I was sure he would think I was crazy, so fear kicked in and killed the thought. I could feel myself getting angry. I wasn't getting angry at him, but I was angry at the fact that *NO ONE SEEMS TO UNDERSTAND ME.*

"Well, that's not important. She said all positive things right?"

"Yes she did. Are you upset?"

"No, you just don't understand." I was quiet for about two minutes. Those two minutes felt like the longest two minutes in the world, but something on television had broken the silence. We began to spark up a conversation about our childhood and we were back to being lovey-dovey with each other. Like always, I dreaded seeing him leave, but as soon as he left I called Sarah.

"Hello, Sarah, this is Jamila. So, how did it go with his reading?"

"It went okay, he doesn't believe in my gift, but other than that it went well."

"So, what did he ask?"

"Jamila, I can't discuss that with you. It is confidential."

I was quiet for about five seconds. I was getting pissed because I wanted to know more about his reading. I had assumed since Sarah and I had become good friends, she wouldn't have any problem with telling me about his reading, but I was wrong. She was professional and I respected that.

"So, when do you want to meet?" I asked her.

"Well, I have so many things coming up in the next few months. Thanksgiving and Christmas are coming up, and our family as well as church have many engagements coming up. Jamila, use this time to get to know him better. Let your love blossom. Things will happen in due time. Meanwhile, don't hesitate to call and talk to me. I'm always here for you. Let nature takes its course with you and him."

"Okay, you enjoy the rest of your day. Bye!" I said in a phony voice.

I was upset because there were so many questions I needed answers to, and I felt that Sarah was putting me to the wayside. I knew she was giving me more time, but more time for what? She was holding back something. There was more to this story than just he and I being soul mates. Whatever it was, it was big. I could feel it. I just wanted to know what it was, but it wasn't the time. *What was it Sarah was keeping from me?* This thought kept playing in my mind. I wanted my way. I wanted to know now!

THE HOLIDAYS

As the months passed by, he and I became inseparable. Our love continued to grow and the bond between us became stronger. Things were going so great between us that he invited Jalon and me to his parents' home for Thanksgiving. The night before Thanksgiving I prepared a cheesecake from scratch. My grandfather shared with me his secret recipe before he passed. Making my grandfather's cheesecake reminded me of the bond between my grandfather and me. I missed him dearly. I knew my cheesecake would make a good impression on his family. I made two cheesecakes that night, one for his home and one for my family. The plan was to say prayer and have conversation with my family until it was time for me to leave and go to his parents' home.

The day of Thanksgiving had arrived, and I was helping my mom in the kitchen when I had received the call.

"Hello?"

"Good morning, my sunshine."

"Good morning, my prince."

"How are things going? How did the cheesecakes turn out?"

"Oh, they are perfect!"

"So, when are you and Jalon coming over?"

"I was thinking about 5:30 p.m., because my family is eating at 3:00 p.m. That gives me time with my family and then we will be on our way."

"Oh, okay," he said. "There is something I want to tell you."

"What's going on?"

"I can't fight it anymore, so I'm just going to tell you."

"Tell me what?" *For this man's sake, God, I pray he doesn't have a skeleton in his closet that will jeopardize our relationship. I don't have time for the drama.* There was a ten-second silence on the phone. "Hello? What it is? What do you have to tell me?" Again he wouldn't say anything, and at that point I knew it was something disappointing. "Could you please tell me what's going on?"

"I just wanted to tell you that, I'm so thankful to God that I found you. You are so unique and special to me, and I think it's time for me to tell you." There was a pause again.

"Hello? Tell me."

"I just want you to know that I love you!" My mouth dropped and I got teary-eyed. There was another silence for about ten seconds. "Are you still there?"

"I love you, too. I've been wanted to tell you but I thought it was too soon for me to love someone after only a month and a half. I wasn't sure."

"You know what? I wasn't sure at first but I had to think about my past relationships, plus I just know. I can see myself having a future with you. You are so good to my sons, and I honor that about you. We make a perfect family. I can see myself having a little girl with you. I can't see my life without you."

"Aw, that's so sweet. I feel the same way, and about our little girl who isn't here yet. What would we call her?"

"That's a good question," he answered.

"What about Imani? Imani means faith. I have faith that our love will never die."

"That's a perfect name," he added.

TWO OF A KIND

Thanksgiving dinner with his family was nice. He has six brothers and sisters. The food was good, and they loved the cheesecake. We talked and laughed. His family was so down-to-earth. A month passed, and we spent Christmas together as a family at my mother's house. Jalon and the boys had plenty of gifts. We also spent New Year's Eve with each other. We threw Jalon and the boys a New Year's Eve Party. It was just the five of us but we had a ball. On New Year's Day, we dropped off the kids at their other parents' houses. The boys went home with their mother, and Jalon went over to his father's house.

At last it was just he and I. We had reservations at one of the hotels in downtown Chicago, where we stayed for two nights. We went to the movies and I made us a romantic dinner for two in our room the first night. The next morning I prepared our dinner. I made baked tilapia and potatoes with mixed vegetables on the side. I had packed everything up including my mother's white elegant tablecloth, along with the red and white artificial rose petals. When the night had arrived for our romantic dinner, I made him go to the hotel lobby while I set everything up. I warmed up the food in the hotel microwave and spread the tablecloth over the hotel table. I made sure the table was in front of the window so we could have a beautiful view of downtown Chicago. All the lights from the buildings and the street added to the romantic atmosphere I was creating. To top it off, I had brought this black lace lingerie piece with some black heels. I put on my trench coat so he couldn't see underneath. The plan was for to me to come to the lobby to get him.

As I walked down to the lobby, I saw him sitting on the couch talking to someone, but the pole was blocking my view of whom he was talking to. As I got closer, I saw that he was talking to this tall black beautiful woman. Immediately, my face dropped and I could feel my blood begin to boil. I was pissed. When he saw my face, he got up and introduced me to the woman. I didn't care who she was; I was pissed.

"Are you ready?" I tried to say politely, but he could tell something was wrong as we walked to the elevator. "Is there anything wrong, Jamila?"

"I'm gonna get right to the point. How long where you talking to that woman?"

"Not long, she was waiting for her husband to come down…"

"Damn, you must have been talking with her for a long time if you know all that about this woman." He tried to change the subject.

"So, what's under this coat?" He grabbed me from behind, but I yanked from him.

"So, what did you guys talk about? It seemed like you guys were enjoying yourselves. Smiling and shit. For future reference, if you want to flirt with another woman, make it on your own damn time when I'm not around."

"Wait a minute, wait a minute, Jamila. It wasn't like that at all. I would never flirt with another woman in your presence."

"So, you would wait to do it behind my back, just like a man."

"Jamila, snap out of it. It wasn't like that. I'm ready to eat. Is everything ready?" Finally, we arrived at our room. "Oh, wow, Jamila, this is so nice. Wow, you have taste. Everything smells good. Why do you still have the coat on?"

"And I'm not taking it off. Maybe you should go back downstairs and entertain your friend."

"Jamila, you are not going to let that go". I could tell he was getting impatient with my temper. "You know what? I'll wait here until you calm down."

"Why wait! Go downstairs with your home girl!" He didn' respond. The room was silent for about a good fifteen minutes. Then I finally calmed down and realized how petty I was being.

"Are you mad?" I asked. He looked up with a smile on his face. "I know you are not smiling. What's so funny?"

"You," he said.

"What do you mean? Glad to know that I am amusing you." I was getting pissed all over again.

"You are just like me."

"What do you mean I'm just like you?" I said with a little disgust in my voice.

"You have a jealous streak just like me, but yours is worse. I never thought I would find someone almost identical to me. In my past relationships my jealousy was an issue with the women I dated, but you are worse than me, but I love you anyhow." I began to laugh.

"I'm sorry for that."

"Don't apologize. It's just the way you are, and I accept you the way you are." Finally, I took off the coat and he was stunned. We sat and ate dinner. We talked all night. The night ended perfectly.

Although it had been a couple of months since I had seen Sarah, we talked at least once every week to keep the communication going. More months had gone by and he and I were deeply in love and couldn't anyone or anything break the strong bond between us.

THE EXORCISM

May 20, 2009, was the day I received the call. This call was the beginning of a new life.

"Hello, Jamila, this is Sarah. It is time." I was thinking to myself, *Time for what?* but I didn't ask any questions. All this time there had been more to the story than what she had been telling me. All the pieces to the puzzle were finally coming together, and I was excited because I knew all my questions would be answered. Right after work I rushed over to Sarah's house. As we sat down, I couldn't stop smiling.

"Jamila, I called you over here because the time has come for you to know the truth," she said as she looked into my eyes with a serious look.

"Truth about what?" I said confusedly.

"The truth of why you are in so much pain most of the time. The truth and cause of your confusion. The truth of why your writing career hasn't been successful. The truth of why you can't seem to get out of this financial rut. As I speak, you can ask questions in the process. I have to be careful of what I say to you and how I answer your questions because he's listening to every word. Are you ready?"

I didn't know for what, but curiosity kept me interested. I whispered, "Who is listening?" I didn't have a clue what she was talking about. "I'm ready."

"The woman at the store, the woman at the job, the woman in the attic.

"What? What are you talking about?" She didn't respond.

"Who are all those women?" I asked again. "So you are telling me that he is cheating with all these women?" Again, no answer from Sarah. "I knew it; I knew it was too good to be true. All men cheat and they are dogs."

Sarah looked down. It was like she was talking in code, but because I was in this old state of mind, I couldn't decipher the information she was giving me, but she knew slowly but surely over time I would figure it out. I was in disgust. She continued.

"He is a liar! Kick him out! He has betrayed you," she said. "Do something exciting you are so boring. Go rob a bank run away and don't come back. They don't love you. You are weak." I was ready to run out of Sarah house, but something kept me there. I wanted to cry, but my pride wouldn't let me.

"Why is he doing this?" I said with my head down. "Why did God put me together with my soul mate if it wasn't meant to be? I am so tired of being treated this way." After hearing these disappointing words, my heart sunk to the bottom of my stomach.

Sarah continued. This time she began to describe an environment. "The walls are white, everyone is looking at you, but you are talking to yourself. Everything is clear now. You scream and scream. All the guilt and pain is removed and the tears are running down; you feel different and alone. You've been chosen."

"Chosen for what?" Again, no response. I was pissed and hurt a bad combination for me.

She continued. "His soul is crying out. He needs you to free him."

"What? Is he in jail?" She let out a little giggle. I didn't know what was going on. She was saying all this stuff but it didn't make any sense. She continued to describe different situations and events. After she was done, I began to ask all the questions I needed answers to.

"What were you describing?" I asked.

"The first description was your negative thoughts."

"Were my thoughts true about him?"

"That depends on him."

"What?"

"You are being controlled"!

"Who is controlling me?"

"Negative forces! Jamila, it's okay. Do not be afraid." I was upset and didn't know what the hell was going on, but the things she was telling me were sounding crazy, and I had begun to think maybe she was playing a game on me or something.

"What did you mean when you said 'his soul is crying out'?"

"Someone is trying to get a message to you."

"Who!" I replied. She wouldn't answer. "You said I could ask questions and that you would answer them, so why will you only answer some of the questions and not all?" I was ready to walk out on her, but I wanted to hear more.

"I also told you that I had to be very careful of what I've saying because we are being listened to."

"Okay, whatever. So you are telling me that I'm being controlled by demons?"

"Yes, you have sided with Satan and you haven't realized it, but something in you knew something was wrong." I put my head down with shame and a tear rolled down my face.

"No, do not be too hard on yourself," Sarah said. "Most, or maybe all, people don't know that they are being controlled. Something deep inside you led you to feel something was wrong, and you asked God for help. We crossed paths for a reason, but you can be free. You can be free of that heaviness in your chest. You can set your spirit free and return on God's side."

"How can I do that? How can I be right with God again?" I knew I was angry with God, but I didn't know I was serving on the wrong side. I was heartbroken and I was willing to do anything to get right with God again.

"We can say a prayer." I stood up and we prayed. After we prayed, she took out a weird object. It was about twelve inches long and it was oval-shaped with small holes in it.

"I'm going to speak in a language you don't understand. Don't be afraid."

She began to shake the object around me. There was something in the object being shaken; it sounded like sand. I remember the smell of incense burning. As she shook the object around me she began to speak in a crazy language. I was trying so hard not to be afraid, but sometimes we are scared of things we don't understand. This act had taken about a good two minutes. After we were done, she gave me a bag. When I felt the bag it felt like a bag of sand.

"Whatever you do, be careful with this bag do not open it. Now, I want you to dump this bag in a dumpster. Put it in a dumpster away from your house, and go a different route home."

I wanted to know why we were doing this, but deep inside I knew this was just the beginning.

"Jamila," she continued, "I want you to come see me tomorrow right after work. There is more we have to talk about. Do not tell anyone what we did or talked about today."

"Okay!" I took the bag and did what I was told. I couldn't wait until I could talk to him. As usual we talked all night until I fell asleep, but I never mentioned my meeting with Sarah.

The next morning I woke up with a smile on my face, and I was so eager to go over Sarah's house. Today was the day she and I would further talk. There was more she had to tell me.

As usual, the day at work dragged by, but I didn't mind because I was able to see him. His birthday was this weekend and I had everything planned. I didn't have a lot of money, but I was going to make his birthday memorable. Before I knew it the day ended, and he and I said our good-byes. I rushed to my car and drove to Sarah's house. She lived only three blocks from my job, so it didn't take me long to get there.

"Hi, Jamila, how do you feel?" She had directed me to a small room with two small chairs.

"Am I supposed to feel different? Now that you say something, I do feel a little different. I feel lighter and I don't have that tightness in my chest anymore."

"Good, now there is more I need to tell you, and then you can ask all the questions you want."

"Are you going to answer all of them?"

She smiled. "It depends. Like I said, we are being carefully listened to."

"Okay, I'm ready," I said impatiently.

"Jamila, now that you have gotten help, Satan is going to attack you. You are a threat to him and his kingdom."

"Me! What's so special about me?"

"Do you remember you were telling me about your writing? Your science fiction plays about God and Satan and the war. It is not science fiction. It is true. God has been calling you for a long time since the age of eleven when you began to write. At a very young age, you knew so much and you were strong in the eyes of God.

"Well, what happened?"

"Since the day you were born on this earth, Satan has been trying to destroy you. He's worked through people around you to hurt you and keep you controlled. He has used your past hurt to get you to turn your back on God and join his hell on earth. You have been bombarded with so much negativity in your life that it has affected your mindset, but now all that will change. Now, once it is time you will hear a voice. Listen; don't act. Remember, Jamila: listen; don't act. Satan will intervene and try to make you think that you are crazy, but you are not. You have a beautiful mind and that is your gift. Since you were a little girl you have seen things that people around you can't see. You remember!"

"Yes, I do; I remember." As soon as she said that I knew what she was talking about. "Yes, I was about five or six years old and I saw these colors red, black, purple, and yellow, and I could see them shaking, like they were vibrating, and they formed a ball and inside that ball were numerous eyes. I was lying next to my mother and when I had told her what I had seen, she rushed me to the hospital. I never opened my mouth about what I saw again. I thought something was wrong with me, and so I suppressed it, but recently about six months ago I began seeing the vibrations and the balls of eyes again. What are they?"

"Your mind is very unique and there is no one on earth with the same mind as you. This is your gift, your mind." Although what she was saying sounded crazy, it was true because I felt it.

"You have to pay attention to that feeling in your chest. You feel the energy of other people, as well as demons and angels. You can sense when they are around.

Now, I am going to tell you what I see. You ready?"

"Yes!"

"The woman in the attic, the woman at the store, the woman at the job. He lives a life of lies and deception. KICK HIM OUT!"

"What! Is he cheating?"

"No, Jamila. Listen; don't act. These are people who are in need of help. These spirits are hindered and they are crying out to be freed."

"And who is going to free them?"

"You are."

"How?"

"In due time you will figure it out."

"Why did the voice say, 'Kick him out'?"

"That was the serpent. He is going to try to deceive you. He doesn't want you and him together."

"Why?"

"You both are a threat to Satan's kingdom on earth."

"Am I going to kick him out?"

"Yes."

"Why?"

"Because you don't understand what is going on. You don't know how to decipher what you see in your visions yet or what comes to your mind. Plus, Satan is trying to make it seem like you're crazy."

"What next?""

"Hospital."

"What? Is it the mental institution?"

"Yes."

"Wow, I dreamed that there was a lady in the mental institution. She was screaming."

"That is you," she said. I looked at her in denial.

"Why am I in the mental institution?"

"You didn't understand what was going on and it frightened you. Don't let Satan think you are crazy. You are not crazy."

"What happened to me in the hospital?"

"You were screaming and screaming. He was cleaning you from your pain and guilt. In order for him to use you, you have to be cleansed." "Who is he?

"God, Jamila."

"Use me for what?"

"He will reveal it to you in time. Your vision will change." she continued.

"What do you mean 'change'?"

"In due time, you will know. You will help change the world. Soon you will have the cars you want and the money you want."

"What do you mean 'change the world'?"

"You will change the world with your words. You both are going to live happy and prosperous lives as Christians. You will work for God."

"What! What are you talking about?"

She smiled and refused to answer the question. "Over time you will put everything together and you will know what happened at the hospital and you will know your life's purpose."

"Okay, that's it. I am not a Christian and I never will be. I believe in one God, but I don't believe in everything that Christians believe. I don't believe Jesus was the son of God. He was only a prophet. I don't need Jesus. I can go straight to God. I think you have misread me, because what you just told me will never come true. I don't see it. I just don't see it!"

She looked disappointed, and said, "This is not your true self. Over time you will develop into your true self." I sighed and was ready to leave. "You are going to drive by here about six times."

"Why am I going to drive by your house six times?"

"Your gift is your mind, but Satan will intervene and make it seem like you are crazy."

"Why would God let Satan intervene?"

"Because what you have and are about to experience has to be shared with the world. It is part of your destiny."

"Share what!"

"You will share with the world your experience, this experience, right now at this moment, this conversation and everything that goes along with it."

She wasn't making any sense. I really began she was a hypocrite, just trying to play a game on me. This lady is crazy, I said to myself.

"When you leave here today, you will not remember this conversation until it is time for you to write it."

Finally, the weird conversation was over and I left her house with an attitude. I wanted to curse her out for wasting my time. However, all I could think about was his birthday. I had a romantic celebration planned and I couldn't wait until tomorrow. *He's going to be so surprised, I said to myself.*

STIRRING UP THE GIFT

The next day had arrived and Sarah was right—I couldn't recall anything from the previous conversation we had. My mind was too busy and focused on making this day a perfect day for him—decorations, gift, and at 10 a.m. pick up the cake. I packed up everything and he arrived at the house just in time.

"Good morning, Sunshine," he said as he entered the door.

"Good morning, my prince." "Where's Jalon?" he asked.

"He's with his dad for the weekend."

"Oh, are you ready?"

"Yes, I have to pick up something, and then we can go to our destination."

"Where are we going?"

"I'm not telling you; you know it's a surprise."

We arrived at the International House of Pancakes in Matteson, Illinois, just in time. I made him stay in the car so I could decorate our table. The manager was so nice to me. He gave me a table right away. I decorated the table with a red tablecloth and birthday confetti. I opened the cake and it read "HAPPY BIRTHDAY LOVE JAMILA." I hung up a "Happy Birthday" banner. Everything was perfect. I went to the car to get him. When we walked in, everyone's eyes were on us. It was obvious everywhere we went together that we drew attention to ourselves. As we walked to the table, he saw everything and began to smile.

"Oh, wow, this is so nice of you, Jamila. I love you so much." We sat down and he gave me a kiss, and that was the cue to give him his gift.

"Here, open it." He opened it and was surprised.

"Oh, wow, you got me the watch I wanted. Thank you so much." We ordered our food and we talked about our future together. After a romantic breakfast, we headed toward the movie theater to catch a movie. As the night ended we held each other tight and I listened to his heartbeat. We agreed to see each other tomorrow, which was Sunday and just be in each other's company. We said our good-byes and I watched as he pulled out of the drive. I hated when we departed from each other. The love that was growing between us was just beautiful. Falling in love with this man became one of the highlights of my life, but the first highlight that I will always hold close to my heart was the day I gave birth to my firstborn son, Jalon. What a beautiful spirit he is. Jalon is just like me. He is my genetic replica. Jalon is another me, but in male form. He is truly heaven-sent.

The next morning I felt a little different. My eyesight seemed to be clearer than usual and I didn't feel worried. I felt so relaxed. This was the day the gifts that God blessed me with began to surface. As I started my day, I began to have visions in my mind. I saw a woman at my job and a person from my past relationship. This really startled me. The visions were so clear. I didn't know what was going on. I tried to ignore them but then many more visions came of different high-crimes cities. I was trying to function normally because I didn't want him to recognize the change in my behavior, but he did. We were on our way to the movies and I saw a vision of the man that I was involved with in my past.

"We are going to run into my ex," I said to him.

"How you know?"

"I saw a vision of him."

"A vision?" He looked at me like I was crazy. I couldn't enjoy the movie because I saw another vision of the woman at my job. At the time I couldn't decipher if it was her spirit calling me or if I was having premonitions. I thought I was going crazy, but I was far from it. This was real and it was happening, I just didn't understand what was happening and why. It had gotten worse and worse. I was being bombarded with visions of other people I haven't seen a day in my life. He was getting concerned.

"Are you okay?" he asked, but I didn't respond. I was too busy trying to make sense of what was happening with the visions. I began to cry because I didn't understand what was happening. The visions didn't let up. They continued. He drove me home and insisted that I go lie down and take a nap. I thought maybe God was punishing me. I kept hearing voices of people I knew. It was like their spirit was calling me for what reason, I didn't have a clue, but I wanted it to stop. He stayed around and he periodically came in to check on me while I was sleeping. When I awakened he was lying next to me watching television.

"Do you feel any better?" he asked.

"I feel a little better. Do you mind staying the night with me? I would feel so much better."

"Of course I will." He gently kissed me on the forehead and we continued to watch television until we were both sleeping.

THE TIME HAS COME

My heart was pounding, and my palms were sweating. While sleeping I could feel myself toss and turn. What's going on? I thought to myself. My mind continues to race with these visions. I can't control these thoughts. It was happening again. "Stop! Please stop," I said out loud.

"He lives another life. He lives a life full of lies and deception," the voice said. I could feel a strange eerie feeling in my chest. It was getting stronger and stronger. I was having visions of the woman at the job, the woman at the store, and the woman who lives in the attic. Little did I know, God was showing me the people I was going to help. These people, whoever they were, were my assignments. Their spirits are hindered and I had the power to release their spirits, but before I had begun to understand the reason behind these visions I heard another voice.

This voice was louder than the other voice; plus, the voice sounded familiar. The voice said, "Kick him out. He is a liar and a deceiver. Kick him out now." I jumped out of bed. The voice of Satan had spoken to my mind and twisted my visions to make it seem like he was cheating on me with all of these women. At the time I didn t know any better, so I did what I thought was right.

"Hey! Wake up," I demanded.

"What's wrong, Jamila?" he asked. He jumped out of bed to try to comfort me.

"No, stop! Don't come near me. You've got to go. You live another life. What? You thought that I wouldn't find out?" I said. "Get up and get out!" I began to gather his things. He was startled.

"What's wrong, Jamila?" He looked at me as though he had seen a ghost.

"You are a liar and you have deceived me. I'm tired of all your mind games."

"Jamila, may I ask you a question?"

"No, I knew my visions were right. You ain't shit. All you men are the same." He hurried and gathered his things and left. I was furious. I thought he was cheating based on the visions of all those women. What made me snap was that Satan had me to believe he was cheating with the women in my vision. My mind continued to race.

I looked out of the window to make sure he was gone, but to my surprise he was still in the driveway. I rushed outside. "Why are you still here?"

"Jamila my car won't start. I need a jump."

"Why don't you ask the heifer that you are cheating on me with to come get your ass? Better yet, if you tell that heifer to come on my property I am going to call the police." I was furious.

He pulled out his phone and begun to dial. "I know you are not about to call this woman while I'm standing here," I said while walking toward him.

"Jamila, wait! I'm calling your mother."

"My mother? Why are you calling my mother?"

"Your mother said to come here."

"Oh, wow, is that supposed to scare me you calling my mother? She won't believe your lies." I went inside to see what my mother wanted.

"Yeah, Mom?"

"What's the problem, Jamila?"

"He has been lying to me. He's cheating on me with all these women."

"What women? Do you have proof?" "No, I don"t, but I know, Mom. "Girl, he loves you. Go back to bed." "He needs a jump," I said.

"Jamila, go ask your brother." My brother and his family were visiting us from Las Vegas, and they were sleeping in the other room. It was 3:00 a.m., but I didn't care; I wanted him away from me.

"He needs a jump. Could you please give him a jump? He has to go."

My brother jumped up and went to give him a jump. Meanwhile, those visions hit me again, but this time the visions were more vivid. I had visions of these women again. *Why am I having visions of other women? Some of these women I've never seen a day in my life.* The visions wouldn't stop. I had gone to my room, but I was so scared and uneasy I couldn't go to sleep. I went to see if he had gotten his car started, and I heard him in my mother's room talking to her.

"Why is she doing this?" he asked her. I could see that he almost fell in her arms crying. I felt sorry for him for about a minute, but the other part of me wanted him to leave. My heart wouldn't let me be so cold, so I walked up to him, but he moved away quickly. I could see the fear in his eyes. I stepped back and he left the house. I ran into my room and fell to the ground. What is happening to me? I asked myself. My mind was steadily racing. That night I couldn't sleep, and I refused to go to work in the state of mind I was in. I stayed up that night pacing the floor in my room and receiving these visions of different places and people. He crossed my mind, and I had wondered what he was doing, but whatever was going on with me, I didn't want him to continue to see me like this. I really thought I was losing my mind. My sympathy thoughts of him were interrupted by another vision. This time I visualized him and all my exes from my past controlling everything around. They were using psychic powers to control minds and thoughts of everyone around me and including me, but I was too powerful for them to keep me in bondage. I was the one everyone around me was depending on to free them, free them from being controlled. Most of them didn't have a clue that they were being controlled. I was their savior.

Most of the day had gone by and the visions and thoughts continued. I hadn't slept and I refused to eat anything. I was still trying to figure out what was going on with me. Throughout the visions and thoughts, I remembered what Sarah had told me: "Many people who have this gift all have had their own significant way of recognizing their gift. Your gift is your mind. Remember, Jamila, Satan will try to make you feel like you are crazy." I began to cry because all I wanted was for the visions and vivid thoughts to stop, but they didn't, so I got in my car to go see Sarah. I knocked on her door.

"Hi, Jamila. What's wrong?"

"Something is wrong, I'm having these visions and I don't understand what's happening."

"You look tired, Jamila. Everything is going to be okay." She had a look in her face as though she wanted to explain to me what was happening but she couldn't. I had to go through it.

"Go home and get you some rest, Jamila," she said.

"I kicked him out because of the visions I had of these women. This doesn't make sense. Your voice told me to kick him out."

"I will tell you this that wasn't me. The serpent has intervened, Jamila. Do you want me to call your mother?"

"No!"

"Okay, promise me you will go home and try to get some rest."

"Okay," I said as I looked down in shame. I felt lost and confused. I left Sarah's home and began to drive home. I began to have visions again of different cities nearby. My mind was like a movie playing itself out. It was crazy. Suddenly, I heard a voice.

"You are so boring. Why don't you do something exciting for a change? Quit being scared of excitement. Go rob a bank, run away, go to the airport and get on the plane and go. Do something to put yourself in jail; there is someone there that needs your help. Hurry up and do something. Do something quick. Time is ticking. Drive the car over the bridge."

I was so afraid. Someone was trying to control my mind. I screamed, "Stop! Stop!"

Suddenly, there was another voice. This voice was louder and stronger than the first and it calmly said, "GO HOME." I turned the car around and headed back home. I ran in the house to my room and began to cry.

"What's wrong, Mom?" Jalon said, knocking on my bedroom door.

"I'm okay, Jalon. Tell your grandmother to take you to school. Mom is not feeling well."

"Okay."

"I love you, Jalon."

"I love you, too."

I sat on the floor in my room rocking myself back and forth thinking that this gesture would bring me a little comfort, but nothing worked. Visions were still pouring into my mind. I couldn't control it.

"Jamila, are you okay?" My mother walked in. "Jamila, you are not acting like your normal self. What's going on?"

"I don't know, Mom. It's my mind it's racing and it won't stop. These visions...I don't know."

"I think we should check you into the hospital so they can find out what's going on," she suggested.

"Okay," I agreed and began to get dressed. While I was getting dressed, my mother called my doctor and informed her of my behavior. My mother got the information of what hospital to take me too, and off we went.

Meanwhile, my mind continued to race with visions. While registering in the mental institution, I heard another voice. "You are weak. You will never get through this. You will never win." I began to fight back and talk back. *Why did I do that? I only appear to be even crazier.*

"Shut up. I will get through this. You are not going to win." Just as I was going to sign the registration papers, I heard many more voices cheering me on.

"You can do this. I believe in you. You will make it through this." All I wanted was to make the voices to stop. I screamed, and I refused to sign the papers. Two nurses came toward me and grabbed me by the arms. I was kicking and screaming. I could hear another voice.

"They are going to rape you. We are going to get you." Then I had a vision that I was running through the woods and I was pregnant. He was with me, and we were running toward freedom. My mind continued to race and all I wanted was for it to stop. They took me to a regular hospital room, and as I waited I heard another voice again.

"Scream," it demanded. I didn't respond at first, and then the voice said, "If you don't, I'm going to do something worse to you." I was afraid, so I did everything the voice was told me to do. As I screamed, my mother came to my side to comfort me. I began to have visions of those people who I have hurt and a few of the people who had hurt me. I began to say I was sorry to all those whom I had hurt. I didn't know it at first, but God was cleaning me of my past and guilt just like Sarah had told me. All the nurses kept coming in and out of the room. I overheard them tell my mother that they wanted to do a CAT Scan of my brain, but I refused to corporate. The voice kept telling me that it was going to harm me, so I was terrified for them to do anything to me. However, they strapped me down to the hospital bed and proceeded with the process of the CAT Scan.

"You must be still Ms. Doxy," one of the nurses said.

"I'm coming to get you. You better try to leave," the voice in my head said. I tried to get loose, but I couldn't. I tried and I screamed, but nothing worked. Meanwhile, a man walked into the room and immediately the voice stopped. I could feel this man's energy so strongly. He talked very gently and he told me his name.

"My name is Nurse Tim," he said, showing me his nametag, but his nametag said "Bob." I knew then that it was a sign that God was with me. He stroked my hair and whispered in my ear, "Calm down or they will do more to you. You have to calm down. Everything is all right." For a moment I was calm while this nurse was in the room. It was something about his presence that gave me a sense of peace. As soon as he left, I could hear the voice again.

"You are weak. You will never survive without me," the voice continued. The nurses brought me back to the room with my mother and told her that my room was ready. They were ready to take me to the other part of the hospital. I didn't want her to leave.

"Mom, please doesn't leave."

She looked at me, teary-eyed, and said, "You are going to be okay. I love you, Jamila. Let them find out what's going on with you." She kissed me on the forehead and she left. I was all alone. I thought about him and what he was doing. I missed him so much. The first night in the mental institution wasn't bad. It didn't take me long to sleep since I was given a sleeping pill and medication for hallucinations. At times I could feel the tightness and uneasiness in my chest and my heart rate speeding up. This would happen throughout the day. The second day passed and I hadn't heard from him. My mother had called numerous times and I talked to Jalon a few times, but my heart was broken because I hadn't heard from him.

I stared at the walls while I was in a session. In the session there was a psychologist who talked to the patients about ways of coping with life. I felt that this didn't apply to me because I wasn't stressing about anything. I was simply living my life like I normally did. I wanted to know why did this had happened, but the more I tried to figure it out the more confused I became. Suddenly, a nurse walked in.

"There's a phone call for Jamila Doxy." I jumped up and rushed out of the room towards the phone hoping it was him.

"Hello?" There was a brief silence.

"Hi." It was him. It was him.

"Hi," I said. There was another silence.

"Your mother told me where you were and she gave me the phone number. I needed to hear your voice. I miss you."

"I miss you, too. I'm so happy you called." I had begun to cry.

"I'm coming to see you."

"Okay."

"You have to promise me something, Jamila."

"Yes, what is it?"

"Promise me that you will never talk to that psychic Sarah anymore. She could have done some witchcraft on you or something."

"Okay, I promise. When are you coming up here? I need to see you."

"I'm on my way. Give me an hour."

"Okay, I love you."

"I love you, too. Bye." I hung up the phone and hurried to my room to get my brush so I could look at halfway decent when he arrived.

As I sat in the recreation room waiting for him to arrive, a white man in his mid-thirties sat right next to me. I could feel tightness in my chest. It was so strong. He looked me straight in the eyes and said, "My demon said he will never let me go. All the medicine in the world couldn't defeat me. I am here to stay." When he said this the tightness in my chest became stronger. Immediately, I got up and walked out of the room. That man is crazy, I said to myself. As soon as I began to walk to my room, I looked up and there he was, walking my way. We hugged each other and kissed. We went to my room and we talked about everything else except the event that had taken place two nights before. "When can you go home?"

"I have to stay at least three days."

"Three days! Why?"

"I guess that's a rule for those who are hospitalized in a mental institution."

"Come on. We're gonna get you out of here. I want to talk to a manager to see if you can get to go home tomorrow or something. You feel okay, right?"

"Yes, I'm fine." He finally found the head nurse and he tried everything to convince the nurse I was fine to go home, but it didn't work. I had to stay, but I wanted to leave so I could be with him. We went back to my room and finished talking. We talked about the things we wanted to do this summer with the boys. Soon it was time for him to leave, and I had to go to another session on learning ways to cope with the obstacles in life. I was so bored at these sessions. I was there physically but my mind was somewhere else. The visions and thoughts continued but they had slowed down so I was able to tolerate them.

At last, the day arrived for me to leave the mental institution, and my mother came to pick me up. I was so happy to be on the other side of those hospital doors. As soon as I got home, I hugged Jalon so tightly. Then I called him to tell him I was at home. He was at the house within an hour.

From that day on, he and I were inseparable again. When you saw him, I was right there. A year had passed and we were still in love. We agreed to move in together and start a family together. We couldn't stand to be away from each other. We wanted to wake up to each other every morning. The plan was for us to get a place, get married and then think about having more children. We wanted to have a little girl. Even though our baby girl wasn't here yet, we began to speak about her like she was already in the world. We gave her the name Imani.

A month later, he surprised me and took me to the west side of Chicago to a friend's house. We were going to pick out a puppy. Before we had gotten on the expressway, I had a déjà vu moment. I had dreamed that particular moment before of us driving to the west side of Chicago. Immediately I knew what puppy we would pick and the puppy's name. I smiled. Our puppy was only two months old, but he had some big paws. He was a German Shepherd mixed with a pit bull. What a mixture, but I didn't care. He stole my heart the first time I saw him. I named him Jet.

A NEW BEGINNING

Months had passed and I became sick. In the mornings, I was very sick. I was nauseous all the time. I didn't think I was pregnant because we had had several false alarms, but on New Year's Day 2009 at the hotel in downtown Chicago, the sickness had gotten worse. That was a traditional of ours. We always spent New Year's Day downtown, and we would spend New Year's Eve with the boys. New Year's Day was our day. I remember staring in the mirror in the bathroom of the hotel saying to myself "I'm pregnant." I held my stomach and I began to cry. All the other times I wasn't sure, but this time I was definitely sure. Continuing to rub my stomach, I smiled and looked up and said "Thank you, God."

"Are you ready?" His knock on the door startled me.

"The show starts in about thirty minutes."

"I will be out in a minute."

"Are you sure you okay?"

"Yes, I'm fine." I wanted to tell him the good news but I wanted to be sure so I planned to go to South Suburban free clinic and take a pregnancy test. I wiped the tears from face and we headed to the movies. I, of course, slept through the whole movie.

We checked out of the hotel on a Sunday. We said our good-byes and departed. That evening I called him. I was too excited, plus I wanted to hear his response of the good news.

"I have something to tell you."

"Okay, Jamila, come on and tell me."

"I'm pregnant!"

"Yeah, right, how you know?"

"I just really know this time. I'm going to take off of work and I'm going to the clinic tomorrow."

"Please call you me as soon as you arrive and as soon as you know."

"Okay, I'm so tired. I'm going to go to bed. I will call you as soon as I leave the house."

"Okay, I love you."

The next morning I woke up sick again, and this time I didn't have the urge to eat anything. I called him when I got to the clinic. I waited for about an hour until my name was called. They gave a container to pee in. It was only about fifteen minutes until the nurse came in to read my results.

"Well, Ms. Doxy, you are definitely pregnant. You are six weeks pregnant, and your estimated due date is August 30. "Thank you!" All I could do was smile. I was so happy. I called him as soon as I had got to the car.

"It's positive. I have the paperwork." He was quiet for a moment. I guess he had to face reality. He came over as soon as he had left work. He knelt down and kissed my stomach.

"I hope it's Imani, my little girl," he said.

"Me too. I pray it's a girl."

Now that we had a family dog and were expecting, we needed a place to stay together as a family. The home search had become a headache. One month became months, then a year.

One day when we were driving down Sauk Trail in Park Forest, Illinois, he saw a sign that read "Open House."

We were coming from an appointment with an apartment complex and we had been turned down to rent an apartment. We followed the "Open House" sign and parked our car and walked in. The house was beautiful. It was a two-bedroom and the asking price was $80,000. The real estate agent had told us about another open house on the next block, which was Mohawk. We hurried back in the car and drove to Mohawk. This house was beautiful also. No work needed to be done, unlike the previous houses we visited which needed work on them, but this house was a beauty. The real estate agent gave us a brief history about the home and, sadly, the young woman who was living there died. Even though I didn't know her, I felt sorrow in my heart. I hated to hear about the death of individuals who had a good heart. By the feel of the house, I could tell she had a good heart.

He talked to the real estate agent while I walked around. The place had beautiful hardwood floors. The bedrooms were beautiful. I fell in love with the place, just for a brief moment because of previous experiences. We might get out-bid or someone else will get the house. However, we left feeling so excited.

"Jamila, we are going to try to get this house. It's only going for $67,000."

"Really? Yeah we can try."

"Naw, we are going to get that house. Look at me.

We are going to get this house. You don't worry about it. You've been looking and looking for us, plus you're pregnant. You don't need this stress. It's not good for my baby. I'll do the footwork. You give me all the contact and I will call your brother to see if he can help. Don't you worry about it. I promise I will get us this house."

"Okay, honey, do your thang because I'm tired." My brother and his wife are real estate agents. They had moved to Las Vegas, but they still had contacts in Chicago that would help us. He kept his promise. After we saw the house in April, we closed on the property on May 28, 2010. I was so happy.

The day we moved in our two-bedroom paradise was the day I began to experience and remember what Sarah had told me. Slowly but surely the conversation Sarah and I had had began to surface in my mind. I remember the day I saw them again. Ever since I had been a little girl, I could see the vibrations of the earth, and every time I would focus, the vibrations would come together and form this ball. Inside this ball were many eyes. The colors were yellow, red, black, and purple. For many years growing up I thought that what I was seeing was demonic so I suppressed them. I tried to ignore and suppress them again, but nothing worked.

I was sitting at my kitchen table reading my bible one morning and I could feel something rubbing against my back. At first I was startled and I jumped up, but they felt like the feathers of an angel. I thought about calling my best friend Nicole and explaining to her what I saw. She is gifted like I am. We are so much alike and she would be the only person I could talk to about this ball of eyes.

"Nicole, hey girl, I must be trippin' but my eyesight is changing."

"What do you mean?" she asked.

"I see these balls of eyes and the colors of the eyes are yellow, red, and black. I think it is demonic."

"I don't know what that could be but take the oil and anoint your house again and say a prayer asking God to reveal what these eyes mean."

"Okay, I'm going to do that now. I will talk to you later. Bye."

"Bye."

The rest of the day I was uneasy. I needed to know. I had said the prayer and I was waiting for God to reveal to me the truth. The day was coming to an end and still no answer from God. The next morning I woke up at 5:00 a.m., read my bible and prayed the usual. I was interrupted by the phone ringing.

"Hello?"

"Good morning, girl, this is Nicole. Are you ready for this? I have the answer to your question. Last night, I had a vision that those eyes are not demonic at all. They are eyes of angels. In the vision I saw you talking to the eyes. As you were talking to the eyes, an angel appeared. Someone you know. Girl, then I heard some voices chanting, "Healing hands and tiger eyes." It was getting louder and louder. It woke me up out of my sleep."

"Thank you, God. All these years I thought the eyes were demonic. You said you had a vision. I used to have visions of the future, but I don't anymore."

"That's because what you must do is here. You are in the present of your visions now."

"I'm trying to figure out what that is I don't know what it is. What does God want me to do?"

"He will reveal it to you soon. You will know." Nicole is a great friend of mine. Every morning, I thanked God for her.

MR. KHALIL'S ARRIVAL

On August 18, 2010, at 3 a.m. I began to have contractions. At first, I ignored them, but they got stronger and stronger. This was it. It was time for him and me to finally meet our son Khalil.

"Honey, honey, it's time." I was holding my stomach; the contractions were strong. He jumped up, put on his clothes, and grabbed our overnight bag. The hospital was about forty minutes away. We were headed to the hospital, and I had mixed emotions. I was excited and afraid at the same time.

At last we had arrived at the hospital, and he looked so nervous. We both were. The nurse examined me and I was dilated four centimeters, so they kept me. By the minute, the contractions were getting unbearable and I requested to have an epidural. I was content until the residents of the hospital checked me and told me I was eight centimeters. I was so happy. This was moving fast. A few hours had passed and a different resident came in check me and told me I was only five centimeters. By that time I was furious that all these students kept coming in and out, using me as a guinea pig. I then requested that only the doctor would come in my room. No more residences; I had enough.

The doctor checked me, and he said I was only five centimeters.

"What? What the hell are you talking about? They said that I was eight centimeters, and now I'm going backward." I was pissed.

"Sorry for the misunderstanding, but you are only five centimeters and the baby's heart rate is dropping. We are going to have to do a cesarean. I was terrified when I heard the word "cesarean." I had heard so many horror stories concerning women who had cesarean births.

"I do not want a cesarean!" I screamed.

"I will let you talk it over with your husband," the doctor said.

"Honey, I'm having a cesarean."

"Well, honey, we have to think of the well-being of the baby." I began to cry hysterically. During my meltdown a nurse walked in.

"Hi, my name is Laura, and is it okay for me to ask you a couple of questions?"

"Yes."

"Is this your first pregnancy?"

"No, I have an eight-year-old son."

"Did you have him vaginally?"

"Yes."

"Well, then there is no need for you to panic. We are going to get this baby out vaginally."

"I know, that's right! That's what I want to hear," I said.

"Now, Mom, it's going to take some hard work, but we have to get him out quickly. I'm going to count to three and that is your cue to push. Okay?"

"Okay, that's works for me."

"One, two, three, PUSH!" I don't know what it was about the presence of this woman, but she had given me hope and energy to push. Before I knew it I was pushing, pushing, and pushing with every contraction.

Meanwhile, my epidural had worn off and I had begun to feel everything. I was screaming, and he was screaming, "Get it out, get it out!" It was pretty intense in there.

"Go get the doctor. The baby is ready," Nurse Laura said. "One more push, Mom." The doctor came in and instructed me to push, and out came Khalil Doxy with a head full of hair. He was eight pounds and six ounces, and twenty inches long. I held him in my arms and he broke down and cried. It was a beautiful moment. If it weren't for a nurse named Laura, I would have undergone a terrified cesarean.

One of the worst experiences that a woman can encounter is to have to leave the hospital without her baby. I was heartbroken. Khalil had jaundice and he had to stay under the light for about a week. I went to see him every day. I cried myself to sleep every night until one morning the nurse called and said, "Baby boy Khalil is ready to come home." I was so overjoyed.

Being an at-home mom required an enormous amount of work. I used to think that at-home moms were lazy. I thought they had it easy, but boy, was I dead wrong. Being an at-home mom was no joke. I found out that there wasn't enough time in the day for me to do what I needed to do. I learned that those rich successful men had a superior support system, and that support system was the wife or woman of the man. The woman is so important. She sets the tone for her household. She is the heart of the family.

There were times I had to go in the washroom and sit on the toilet and cry. I looked forward to when he would come home. I didn't want to be alone, but I had an angel to come to my rescue. My friend Nicole came to help me around the house and with Khalil. I am so blessed to have a friend like her. She was truly a good help. She had me prioritize my chores on different days. Friday was my wash day, and I cleaned the kitchen and living room on Mondays. I cleaned the rest of the house on Wednesday. I had to realize that I couldn't do everything in one day. It was impossible. That transition wasn't easy, but soon I adjusted, and to be honest, I still am.

Months passed and I began to remember what had happened to me in the hospital. The word "exorcism" came to mind. I began to hear the voice of Sarah revealing to me our last conversation. I began to have visions of me being in the hospital. The word "demons" came to mind. Even though the incident happened three years ago, over the years it has played in my mind over and over again. He and I never discussed what happened that night when I kicked him out. I didn't know what to think of that incident, so I asked God to reveal to me the truth.

CALLING

The day God revealed to me the truth, I was driving listening to a gospel CD and there was a song titled "Something about the Name Jesus." As I began to sing the song, I could feel the Holy Ghost come upon me. I'd never caught the Holy Ghost a day in my life. For years I never thought it was real, until that day. Suddenly, I began to cry hysterically and thank God for saving me. I rushed home and when I got home, I fell on my knees and God had revealed to me that I was possessed with the demon of fear. God had sent Sarah to release me from the world of darkness. From that day on, I continued to get up and read my bible. I had begun to read a bible that I had gotten from a neighborhood hospital that I stayed at. It was the New Testament with the Psalms. This bible was published by a group called the Gideons International. As I began to read and study the New Testament, my vision changed drastically. It was like a newborn baby when it first sees the world around it; everything is new. I began to see these wavy lines and a glowing aura around me.

I called Nicole to inform her of my changes, and she suggested I rent the movie *The Passion of Christ* by Mel Gibson. She instructed me to ask God to open my spiritual eye to the truth before I viewed the movie and I did just that. As I watched the movie, I periodically felt chills run through my body. When Jesus was being tormented by his own people, more and more chills ran through my body. I cried and these words played in my mind: "I don't believe Jesus was the son of God. He was only a prophet. Why do I have to pray to Jesus to get to God? That's too much red tape. I will cut Jesus if I have to. I'm God." God was replaying to me all the blasphemous and hurtful things I said about Jesus, and I heard them in my mind loud and clear. My stomach turned and I dropped to my knees and screamed and cried out, "I'm sorry, Jesus. I'm sorry, my Lord." I cried on and off for about a week.

I testified to my mother and she told me that I should talk to Reverend Knox from our church. I called Reverend Knox and told her to meet me at my mom's house with my sister, my mom, Nicole, and my niece. I told Reverend Knox about the eyes of angels, the glowing aura and the wavy lines. The day I was to meet with her, my mind began to race and Satan began to play games with my mind. He projected things in my mind nonsense things. I couldn't concentrate. These negative thoughts continued throughout the meeting with Reverend Knox. She and her husband kept their eyes on me. I was there physically but my mind was being played with by Satan. Satan also projected noises in my mind to drive me crazy. I couldn't focus. As Reverend Knox talked, I felt a warmth on my face. I became focused. I turned to Nicole and said, "Girl, I think God just smacked me."

She laughed and said, "No, Jamila, God is letting you know he is here with you. There is something you are ordained to do."

"Well what is it?" I said.

"He will tell you in due time."

When the meeting was over those thoughts continued, and by the end of the day I was exhausted.

On January 12, 2011, at 1:30 a.m., I finally defeated the demon of fear. I had slept so well that night because the last two nights I had a rough time sleeping due to this battle going on in my mind; plus, Khalil waking up to be breast fed didn't make it any better. I heard loud footsteps. I jumped up. I could feel the spirit of fear all around. I began to fight back. "No more," I said. I grabbed my anointing oil and repeated these words: "I rebuke you in the name of Jesus." I stood up tall and told the spirit of fear to get out of my house. I got in the bed and sprinkled oil all around him and me. I also put some around Khalil's crib and on the door of Jalon's room.

I couldn't sleep, and at 6:30 a.m. I informed Rev. Knox of the footsteps I heard, and she told me I was in spiritual warfare and that I was doing great. "When you come out of it, you will be like gold," she said. She told me to get some rest. My mother came over to watch Khalil while I slept.

On January 13, I was filled with the Holy Spirit. A prophet revealed to me that the glowing aura I was seeing around me was actually the supernatural fire of the Holy Spirit. As I began to grow closer to Jesus, my faith became stronger. Being in the presence of God is the most rewarding gift a human being can have. It is a gift I will never give up for all the riches in the world. I had begun to watch Joyce Meyer and Joel Osteen. I favored Joyce because she is a woman. *No offense, Joel.* As I watched her speak, the Holy Spirit began to stir around in me. *She is making such a positive impact on people around the world*, I thought to myself.

"It is time to share your story with the world." The Lord had spoken.

"But I've never written a book before, Lord, just plays. How do I go about writing and who is going to publish it?" I began to panic a little.

"Don't worry about it. I got yo back," the voice said.

I jumped up and said, "I rebuke you, Satan; I rebuke you."

"Jamila, it's me; it is I."

"Who is 'me'?" I asked.

"Jesus."

"Jesus, what are you doing talking like that?" I said.

"Remember I was on earth before and I am here now; therefore, I can relate to you," Jesus said. Tears rolled down my face. "I was there in the hospital room when you were in the mental institution. I was the male nurse. I was there with you." I cried tears of joy.

The next morning I woke up with so much joy in my heart. I picked up my bible and held it in one hand and prayed.

"God, guide my hands to the scripture you want me to read. Speak to me through your word. In Jesus' name, I pray. Amen." When I opened the bible he guided me to 1 Timothy 4:5. The words that stood out, I underlined. I could feel the spirit guiding my hands. When I was done, I read what I had underlined. In 1 Timothy 4:6 "...you will be a good minister of Jesus Christ nourished in the words of faith and of the good doctrine which you have carefully followed. For bodily exercise profits a little, but godliness is profitable for all things, having promise of the life that now is and of that which is to come. Let no one despise your youth, but be example to the believers in word, in conduct, in love, in spirit, in faith, in purity. Do not neglect the gift that is in you, which was given to you by prophecy with the laying on of the hands of the eldership. Meditate on these things; give yourself entirely to them that your progress may be evident to all. Take heed to yourself and to the doctrine. Continue in them, for doing this you will save both yourself and those who hear you."

"Turn to Hebrews chapter one," God instructed me.

The word stood out. Hebrews 1:7: "And of the angels He says: Who makes His Angels spirits and His Ministers a flame of fire." After reading the scriptures in His word, I realized that God was giving me a message through his word.

"Remember, Jamila, I chose you; you didn't choose me. Now it is time for you to speak the truth.

You've been quiet for too long."

"Lord, I am honored and forever thankful that you chose me. I love you dearly. You won't be disappointed." *My teacher says my time is at hand.*

THE BREAKUP

God had prepared me before it took place our breakup that is. I knew it was coming and when it almost came a few times I chickened out because I didn't want to let him go, but I couldn't take the selfishness. I had to let go. I was waiting for him to leave but God put it on my heart that he wasn't going to leave. I had two choices. One: Be taken for granted; or two: Kick him out into the hands of GOD. I chose number two. I would like to say we had an easy breakup but it wasn't easy. It was a good thing nobody was hurt physically, but I can't say that emotionally. Out of anger and hurt, I said some hurtful things to him that I now regret. Emotions are so strong when you are in love.

When he left I was heart-broken and I could feel heaviness and sharp pain in my heart. Again, I was suffering from another broken heart. But this wasn't an ordinary heartbreak; this was worse than all the rest. The excruciating hurt resided within attacking my thoughts with fear of the future. I lost focus of what God chose for me to do: Doing God's will of writing and speaking the truth was the least of my worries. The thought of him consumed my every thought. How could he take me for granted? I thought to myself. I felt used. All the things I had done for him and his children were out of the pureness of my heart. That same night it was difficult for me to sleep. I cried and cried the whole night, but I could feel the presence of Jesus comforting me. Jesus touched my cheek and whispered to my heart, "This too shall pass."

Two weeks after the breakup, the sharp pain and heaviness in my chest was gone. Although the physical effect of the heartbreak was gone, I was still in emotional turmoil. Not only was I in emotional turmoil, Satan was sending negative forces to my mind left and right. Fighting for my mind became an exhausting task until I felt physically beat. I was on an emotional roller coaster for about three months. In the second month God had made me more aware of the condition of the world. Tears ran down my face as I began to think about all of the lost souls. That night I had a dream that Jesus was talking to my spirit and I screamed, "Why?" Jesus and I had a conversation but I couldn't remember it, but I know I was talking to him. In the third month I got fed up with the emotional roller coaster. I got tired of letting people and the negative forces jerk my emotional chain. I wanted a closer walk with God. Although I was in a storm, I disciplined myself to get up every morning at 5:00 a.m. and read and study my bible and listen to inspirational teaching tapes by Joyce Meyer and Johnnie Coleman.

Time had passed and I was still thinking about our breakup. I missed him so much. When God brought us together we were the same, but God had changed me, and God sent me to him because he lived a life of lies and deception. I didn't understand at first, but it all started to make sense. The visions I had had before I met him were real and God had sent me into his life for a reason. At the same time God was teaching me how to love unconditionally and how to let go. I feel women feel we are suppose to love regardless of what people do to us, but we are supposed to love from afar for those who continually hurt us. The fourth month after our breakup, I could feel the presence of Jesus all around. Jesus and I became so close. I talked to him about everything. He was there when I hurt the most. When my friends and family weren't anywhere to be found to confide in or talk to, Jesus was right there to listen and comfort me. When he was near, my heart rate sped up and I felt a warmth that was so comforting. At this moment as I am typing these very words, I can feel his presence. For about a month now he's been pushing me to finish this book. I had lost focus. Well now I have my focus back. He is right here with me and I am forever thankful for his love and support.

On October 22, 2011, I confronted my ex about the hurt that he had caused me. It had been four months since our breakup and lately I had been lashing out at him with harsh words. God revealed to me that I hadn't really forgiven him in my heart. I could no longer carry him in my heart. I had to release him spiritually now. Before he had arrived at the house, I asked Jesus to stay right by my side because of my temper when it comes to my ex. I greeted him with a smile and asked him to step into the kitchen so we could talk.

"Hi, how are you doing?" I said in a calm voice, smiling.

"I'm good," he said in a nervous tone. He had a frightened look on his face, but he tried all his might to cover the hurt that I saw in his eyes.

"I just have to tell you that I am truly hurt. God had given me a beautiful vision of our future and you took that vision and crushed it, and when you crushed it, you crushed a piece of my heart. However, I forgive you, but I had to get this off my chest and leave it with you because it would not be fair to the next man that comes into my life, and this man is going to be something else because he will be a man from God, and I finally know the difference. I also want you to forgive me for using harsh words when I communicate with you, but I'm hurt."

"This is the only bad breakup I've ever had," he said.

"That's because you never had a real woman. You knew what this was," I said getting angry. I could feel Jesus touching me with comfort.

"I know you hurt and I'm hurt too, but we've got to get through it," he replied.

"I'm going to be fine. God's got me," I said confidently. We shook hands and he left. When my ex left, I felt so relieved. It felt like a load had been lifted off my shoulders.

I know you are thinking to yourself, 'I thought this was the end of the book. Me too but God put it on my heart to share this experience.' There I was sitting on my mother's couch angry with God for what just happened. I had just been released from the Ingalls mental institution in Harvey Illinois. I stopped taking my medication. I felt like I was healed, and I didn't need it, but oh boy was I wrong. This rebellious behavior had gone on for about 3 years straight. Like I said I was angry with God. It was the year 2012 and my life seemed like it was going down the toilet. I was diagnosed with schizophrenia bipolar type with major depression. Here I was suffering from a mental Illness, a mother of two beautiful sons, no job, and my home was in foreclosure. I wanted to die. I can't count on my fingers how many times I prayed to God to take my life. I didn't want to face the healing process I was about to go through.

The healing process can be a challenge, but the beginning stages can be unbearable. My mind was in a dimension of hell. I was stuck in the past. I was molested at the age of eight. I was raped in my early twenties. Taking physical and verbal abuse from men became the norm for me. My question was how did I get here? Why did I let those people take advantage of me, especially loved ones? I'm not writing to complain. I'm going to tell you about me.

Let's go back when I was on my mother's couch. I was angry with God and tired of making frequent trips to the mental institution. I remember that particular conversation I had with God. "God my plans are ruin I said in a loud but angry voice". To my surprise a small still voice answered and said. "Your plans are insufficient. From that point on I stopped yelling at God. At that time in my life I was mad at the world. That was the day my healing began. I didn't have a job, so I had all the time in the world to spend with Jesus. I thought to myself, "all the things I been through, the mind can only take so much and here I was. After my brief conversation with God I had to go to my psychiatry appointment. I went to cook county hospital in Chicago, Illinois. My mental health nurse practitioner was Arabic. She was so nice and understanding. I told her I was having crying spells every day, sometimes throughout the day. Then she told me that I suppress my emotions and she was right. I was never taught the proper way to let those emotions out. My mind and body were reacting to all the suppressed emotions of my past, especially the past traumatic events I had experience. I didn't realize that when we as human beings experience the death of a loved one that experience is considered to be a traumatic experience.

The beginning of my healing was scary. I literally felt the stress and trauma in my body. I felt it mainly in my chest. It would sometimes move from my chest to my left or right arm. Occasionally , it would move to my stomach. I tried to soothe this pain by playing gospel music or by just keeping myself busy. Keeping myself busy was my favorite coping skill. However, this so-called coping skill was making the pain worse. I just wanted the pain to stop. I wanted to stop feeling all together. I remember there were days I sat in my foreclosure home trying to fight off anxiety attacks. There were days I couldn't get out of bed. My mom, my angel would come and help me get my two boys ready for school. Whenever I need my mother, she tries to be there for me no matter what. My mother wasn't perfect while raising my sister and brothers', but she always set perfect examples of how to live a spiritual life. How does one live a spiritual life? You rely totally on God and Jesus to take you through life. As a little girl I remember seeing my mother read her bible in the mornings. She would also do vision boards of her goals.

Forgiveness is the beginning of new life. It frees my heart of the wrong choices chosen by others. Yes, it does hurt when others hurt me, especially when it is done intentionally, but their lashing out toward me is only a reflection of the hurt that resides within them. This doesn't give them an excuse for his or her actions, but it frees me from being captive in their world of hell. Jesus is continuing to guide me on how to deal with evil. Day by day he is instructing me on how to live in this world without conforming to the way of this world.

It is shocking how this story ends. What I thought was my ending was just a new beginning of all the things that God has in store for me. The man who I thought was my soul mate was just an assignment to prepare me for my purpose and for me to receive my true soul mate, who will be a man of God. The psychic Sarah had known this but she kept the truth from me. If I knew the truth, that I would have to suffer another heartache, I wouldn't have gone through with it. My assignment with my ex would have been incomplete. Jesus revealed to me that all of those men who thought they succeeded in using me were also being used themselves. God used them to build me into the woman he needs me to be for him. I will be like the sun that will shine forever and never die. Those around me will envy what I have, but the truth is that they can have it also. They will want to know how, and I will tell them *it was Jesus who saved me from a life of hell.*

"EVERY KNEE SHALL BOW AND EVERY TONGUE SHALL CONFESS IN MY NAME (JESUS CHRIST)."